THE GREEN PAGES

YOUR EVERYDAY SHOPPING GUIDE TO ENVIRONMENTALLY SAFE PRODUCTS

THE BENNETT INFORMATION GROUP

Random House
New York

We have compiled our listings based on product labels, information from manufacturers, and catalog descriptions. We have made every effort to ensure accuracy within the limits of these information sources, but cannot guarantee completeness or accuracy in each case. The reader is advised to examine product labels and warnings carefully before purchasing and using to ensure suitability. Follow manufacturers' instructions for use. No endorsement is intended or implied for any product in this book. Finally, we cannot guarantee that any particular item will function according to the claims of the manufacturer.

Random House publications are available at special discounts for corporate use, in bulk purchases of 100 copies or more for promotions or premiums. Special editions, including personalized covers and corporate imprints, can be created in large quantities for special needs. For more information, write to the Director of Special Markets, Random House, Inc., 201 East 50th Street, New York, NY 10022.

Library of Congress Cataloging-in-Publications Data

The green pages: your everyday shopping guide to environmentally safe products/Bennett Information Group
p.cm.
ISBN 0-679-73130-x
1. Environmental protection—Citizen participation.
2. Environmental protection—Equipment and supplies. 3. Household supplies.   4. Consumer education.
I. Bennett Information Group.
TD171.7.G74 1990
363.7'0525—dc20   90-37831

Manufactured in the United States of America

98765432

First Edition

Printed on recycled paper
Cover printed with water-base ink

5/91

Acknowledgments

Many people participated in the creation of this book. Tom Maugh, Dorian Kinder, June LaPointe, Peter Kinder, and Nancy Schmid, all members of The Bennett Information Group, did a splendid job of researching environmental issues and developing product listings (see page 237). Peter Randall, probably the best dBASE programmer in the country, worked hard to write a database program that would accommodate our ever-changing needs. Thanks for your patience, Peter.

Begabati Lennihan helped us identify the best products found in natural food stores. Debra Bottega of Flexel, Inc., taught us a lot about the cellophane industry. Thanks also to the people at the American Paper Institute for providing information about paper recycling. Mike Snell, literary agent for The Bennett Information Group, was instrumental in shaping the book.

We are especially grateful to the people at Random House. Charlotte Mayerson, our editor, worked closely with us during every phase of development and played a tremendous role in shaping the book. She also has the patience of a saint. Thanks also go to Lani Mysak and Cindy Stewart for helping to coordinate details, and to Naomi Osnos and Pat Ehresmann for working with us during production.

Special thanks also go to Beth McMacken, art director of PageWorks, Inc., of Cambridge, Masschusetts, for designing and laying out the book, and Ron Creamer, president of PageWorks, wrote the programs that converted our database listings into final output.

Of course, we thank our friends and family for their patience while we scoured the supermarket aisles, product brochures, and mail-order catalogs to find the most useful information possible.

Contents

The Light at the End of the Tunnel

☞ Green Problems...

Walk the beaches and see the tampon applicators, disposable diapers, syringes, and other debris of modern civilization. Canoe the rivers and see the floating trash bags, soft drink bottles, and six-pack rings. Drive the highways and see the foam hamburger containers, soft drink cups, and coffee cups. Walk the streets and breathe—but not too deeply—the smog, the hydrocarbon fumes, the carbon monoxide. Drink the water and smell the subtle essence of chloroform, taste the tangy bite of acid, and the sweet savor of synthetic fertilizers.

Or go farther from home. Visit the Midwest and feel the heat of the hottest decade on record. Fly over Brazil and view the immense smoke plumes from the burning rainforests. Go farther still, to satellite height, and look down on the ozone hole over Antarctica or the nascent hole over the Arctic.

From the so-called greenhouse effect that threatens to heat the Earth irreversibly to the overflowing landfill down the block, we're confronting a range of environmental problems that no one could have even conceived of 50 years ago. Among the most pressing:

Solid Waste

With only 5 percent of the world's population, the United States uses 25 percent of its resources and generates 30 percent of its garbage. Each American throws away at least 3.5 pounds of garbage per day, a total of more than

150 million tons per year. That amount of trash grew by 60 percent between 1960 and 1986, and some critics predict that the amount of trash discarded per person will grow to more than 6 pounds per day by the turn of the century.

About 5 percent of our trash is recycled and another 10 percent is burned in incinerators, but the bulk goes into an estimated 6,000 landfills around the country. Unfortunately, those landfills are filling up at a rate of about 600 per year, almost faster than we can build new ones. Los Angeles is expected to run out of space for new landfills by 1995, Chicago by 1994. Already, some towns in New England are trucking their solid wastes to Pennsylvania and Ohio, while communities on Long Island, New York, send trash by train as far west as Michigan. Some areas are even considering waste disposal sites in South America and Africa. And then there's the memorable voyage of the *Mobro 4000*, a garbage barge that traveled in vain for more than 5,000 miles, in search of a refuge for its refuse. Eventually, it wound up back where it started, parked in the harbor of New York City.

Even if there were room for all of our trash, much of it contains toxic chemicals that can leach out of landfills and contaminate the groundwater that half of all Americans rely on for drinking water. Environmentalists estimate that the Fresh Kills landfill in New York City leaks approximately 4 million gallons of toxic liquids into nearby streams and groundwater every day—and that's just one example.

Water Pollution

Americans dump 16 tons of sewage sludge into rivers, streams, and the ocean every minute, a total of 8.5 million tons every year. Industry adds another 9.5 million tons of wastes. Both of these totals are dramatically smaller than they were a decade ago, however, as a result of new Federal regulations. Today, a greater concern is "non-point-source pollution"—pesticides and fertilizers from lawns and farms as well as gas, oil, lead, de-icing salts, animal feces, and other materials from city streets. Non-point-source pollution accounts for as much pollution as sewage and industrial wastes combined.

Air Pollution

Six out of every 10 Americans—that is, 146 million—live in areas that do not meet Federal standards for clean air. The U.S. Environmental Protection Agency (EPA) has identified 320 different toxic chemicals in the air, 60 of which are known to cause cancer. Some of these chemicals come from industry: a 1985 Congressional survey of the chemical industry found that 230 facilities in 36 states released about 62 million pounds of toxic chemicals into the air annually.

But the bulk of the 2.4 billion pounds of toxics released every year comes from our ordinary daily activities. About 40 percent of the hydrocarbons that are a crucial component of smog and of acid rain comes from automobiles and trucks—and not only from exhaust gases, but also from fumes released every time you fill your gas tank, every time the gas station's tanks are filled from a tank truck, and every time tankers are filled at the refinery.

In addition, cars and trucks emit significant quantities of carbon monoxide, which causes breathing problems, and nitrogen oxides, which cause health problems and acid rain. Automobile emissions are the single most important source of air pollution. They have been reduced substantially over the past two decades, but those decreases have been more than offset by the 55 percent increase in the number of cars on the road.

Air pollution also comes from solvents from dry cleaners, power mowers, oil-based paints and varnishes, charcoal lighters, and a multitude of other products used around the home.

Acid Rain

While urban air pollution tends to remain fairly localized, acid rain is an air pollution problem that stretches far beyond urban areas. Sulfur dioxide (produced by burning coal and petroleum) and nitrogen oxides (produced by all types of combustion) combine with water vapor in the air to produce particulates of sulfuric and nitric acids, which are spread hundreds of miles by atmospheric patterns. When these acids finally precipitate from the air, the resultant rainfall can be as much as 10,000 times more acidic than ordinary rainfall.

Acid rain has a variety of deleterious effects. It corrodes metals and eats away granite and other stone building materials. A 1985 EPA study found yearly damages totaling $5 billion to houses and other structures in a 17-state area—a figure that does *not* include physical damage to cars or damage to historical and cultural landmarks.

Perhaps more important are acid rain's effects on life. Acid rain weakens trees, making them highly susceptible to bacterial, viral, and fungal infections. Forests around the world have suffered six major "diebacks" since 1978 as a result of air pollution, primarily acid rain. According to the EPA, 50 percent of the red spruce trees at high elevations in the Green Mountains of Vermont have died over the last two decades because of acid rain. Sugar maple trees in the Northeast and Canada are threatened with extinction as a result of acid rain. In the province of Quebec alone, 82 percent of sugar maples have already died or have been seriously damaged.

In lakes and streams, acid rain affects all species. First, the plankton and microscopic organisms that serve as food for larger species die off, causing mass starvation. As the water becomes more acidic, most species of fish stop reproducing. In still more acidic conditions, calcium leaches out of the bones of fish, causing deformities and, eventually, death. When such high levels of acidity are reached, virtually every species dies off. According to a 1988 report by the U.S. Office of Technology Assessment, 3,000 lakes and 23,000 miles of streams in the eastern United States were exceptionally vulnerable to slight increases in acidity or were already barren.

Global Warming

Ice floes at the poles are melting. Ocean levels around the world are rising perceptibly. Many climatologists believe the world is entering an era of temperatures higher than any seen since the Cretaceous period, more than 65 million years ago, when dinosaurs ruled the world. The average surface temperature of the Earth has risen by nearly one degree Fahrenheit since the 1850s, and estimates indicate that it could increase by another eight degrees by the middle of the next century.

The source of this global warming is the greenhouse effect, in which certain atmospheric gases trap heat that

would normally be radiated into space. The most important of these gases, carbon dioxide, accounts for about 60
percent of global warming. The amount of carbon dioxide
in the atmosphere has increased 25 percent since the
beginning of the Industrial Age; estimates based on present growth rates indicate that it will nearly double by the
middle of the next century. The remaining 40 percent of
global warming is caused by a variety of other gases,
including chlorofluorocarbons and nitrogen oxides.

Some scientists believe that global warming may cause
the level of the oceans to rise by as much as 15 feet, inun-
dating large portions of the American coastline and
destroying coastal wetlands that now serve as breeding
grounds for much of the oceans' animal life. Prime agricultural regions in the northern hemisphere would shift
northward across the globe. Weather patterns would also
change significantly, with monsoons becoming more
common and more powerful on the Indian subcontinent
and rainfall decreasing in the U.S. on average. The power
of hurricanes would also increase dramatically.

Ozone Depletion

In addition to global warming is another problem, ozone
depletion. The ozone layer is a wispy layer of gas in the
upper reaches of the atmosphere that screens out virtually all of the sun's damaging ultraviolet radiation. But chlorofluorocarbons—man-made chemicals now used in air
conditioners and refrigerators, for cleaning electronic
equipment, and in making foam insulation—are slowly
destroying the ozone layer.

These lightweight chemicals gradually float up to the
stratosphere, where they destroy ozone molecules.
Researchers believe that the ozone layer has already been
depleted by 1 to 2 percent overall, but some seasonal variations are much greater: over Antarctica an area the size of the
U.S. suffers a 50 percent depletion of ozone for the three
months of the southern hemisphere's spring, a phenomenon
that is now known as the "ozone hole." The beginnings of a
similar hole have been observed over the Arctic.

Ozone depletion will have a variety of effects, none of
them good. One obvious impact will be a significant
increase in the incidence of skin cancer. According to the

EPA, there will be 150 million more cases in the U.S. over the next 80 years if the release of chlorofluorocarbons continues at present rates. The increased ultraviolet radiation will also reduce agricultural productivity by giving plants the botanical equivalent of a bad sunburn. It will kill off microorganisms at the surface of the ocean, thereby decimating the oceans' food chains. Finally, ozone depletion will also change weather patterns, perhaps exacerbating the changes caused by global warming.

In short, the planet is in trouble.

☞ ...And Green Solutions

As bleak as the state of the environment might seem, partly through public pressure, more and more environmental laws are being added to the Federal and state books every year. And manufacturers in many industries are beginning to take environmental concerns more seriously.

Awareness of the poor state of our environment has reached an all-time high—people from all parts of the country are eager to help in the great cleanup ahead. And they can make a small, but important, contribution through modest changes in the way they do their chores, cook their food, and carry on their daily lives.

Pollution in America is a cumulative problem that grows out of the everyday activities of 240 million people. Just as surely as every bit of pollution or waste hurts, every bit of effort made for the environment helps. And those individual efforts accumulate just as fast as the bad effects:

- ◆ If one out of every four households used just 10 fewer plastic bags per month, we would save more than 2.5 billion bags per year.

- ◆ If only 10,000 families installed low-flow aerators on faucets in their kitchens and bathrooms, we would save 33 million gallons of water per year and lighten the load on sewage systems.

- ◆ If just one out of every 65 people whose automobile tires are underinflated would add air, we would save 30 million gallons of gasoline per year.

One of the simplest things that everyone can do to make a difference is to buy "green" products. Green products are designed with the environment in mind. By using them, you'll reduce your contribution to the solid waste problem and decrease the amount of unnecessary chemicals released into our air and water.

Where do you find such products? In your local supermarket, drug store, department store, natural food store, and mail-order sources. But they aren't always easy to identify, and some claims about "environmental friendliness" simply aren't true. (For instance, at this time there's no such thing as a truly biodegradable plastic bag, plastic diaper, or plastic container.)

That's why you need *The Green Pages* to guide you through the store aisles. The book is uniquely designed to help you make purchases that are healthier for the environment *and* meet your needs. Let's see how *The Green Pages* can work for you:

☞ A Guide for the Green Consumer

The Green Pages is divided into three main parts. The first, "The Market Shopper's Guide," is devoted to listings of products that you can readily find in supermarkets and natural food stores. These products range from laundry detergents and food to "baby wipes" and garden supplies. The product listings are organized into eight chapters that encompass the various areas of your household where activities contribute to pollution and other environmental problems are likely to occur:

- ◆ Laundry
- ◆ Broom closet
- ◆ Kitchen
- ◆ Workshop
- ◆ Nursery
- ◆ Yard (including pet products)
- ◆ Bathroom
- ◆ Garage

Each chapter describes the major environmental issues that green consumers should be tackling. The chapters also contain suggestions for simple things you can do to help the environment without seriously affecting your lifestyle—doing full washloads instead of partial loads, using sponges instead of paper towels, and so on. Happily, you'll find that some of the steps that can help save the environment will also save you money.

Each chapter in Part I concludes with our recommended criteria for selecting and purchasing green products, followed by the actual product listings. As you can see in the sample listing shown below, each entry contains the following types of information: Product name, followed by type (liquid, powder, etc.), manufacturer, and description (why it is a green product).

Arm & Hammer **Detergent (Powder)**	*Church & Dwight*	Phosphate-free Chlorine-free Recycled packaging

Part II of The Green Pages, "The Mail-Order Shopper's Guide," lists green products that can be obtained from mail-order catalogs. The product listings in Part II contain one or more numeric codes that correspond to the mail-order catalogs listed in pages 231 to 236 (see the sample listing below).

The mail-order items have been included for those people who do not have access to major supermarkets or natural food stores, or who want to use their automobiles as little as possible in order to reduce their gasoline consumption and contribution to air pollution. In general, these products are made by small manufacturers and reflect a very high degree of concern for the environment in terms of product content and packaging. If you're not accustomed to mail-order shopping, you might want to experiment with a few products, then develop a "mix" of regular supermarket and catalog purchases. That will expose you to products not generally available in stores, and at the same time enable you to maintain your regular shopping routines.

Biobottoms Diaper **Covers (Wool or cotton)** Biobottoms	Natural fiber Biodegradable Reusable/recyclable	55

Since new products are introduced every day and since there are some regional differences, you'll no doubt see in your store some items not listed in this book. But if you've read the chapter introductions and studied the green criteria, you'll be able to make informed buying decisions on your own. In fact, one of the major goals of the book is to provide you with a "green grammar" that enables you to make sound product evaluations for yourself. (See "The Green Label Reader," page 225, for a quick summary of the environmental impact of major ingredients in products.)

To learn more about environmental issues, we suggest that you also read Part III, "A Guide to Environmental Issues." You'll find detailed explanations of topics such as acid rain, biodegradability, and recycling. This will also help you become aware of the relationship between your household and the rest of the world. Sure, a single jar of petroleum jelly purchased for your nursery does not represent a major environmental threat. But when you consider all the people buying petroleum-based products, that adds up to a lot of crude oil being transported by sea (with the attendant risks of spills) and a lot of refineries belching pollutants into the atmosphere. To put it another way, just about everything you do in life has some environmental consequence. Why not try to make it a positive one?

☞ Making Lifestyle Changes

Many people are concerned that buying green means adopting a strict, back-to-nature stance. That's not what we're advocating. Imagine a spectrum: at the one extreme, we continue on our present course, destroying our natural resources and consuming as if we had unlimited landfill capabilities; at the other extreme, we shun all conveniences, technologies, and synthetic materials, and return to simpler times. For the majority of Americans, both extremes are unacceptable: making peace with the environment means undergoing a gradual learning and change process that will lead us to a comfortable and non-destructive way of life.

For instance, if you can't imagine switching to cloth diapers for your baby, try using them one day a week. You'll still be making a positive contribution to the environment. Perhaps, later on, you'll feel comfortable enough to use cloth diapers two days a week, eventually making a complete switch.

If you have a favorite detergent that isn't 100 percent phosphate-free, try using a phosphate-free brand for every fifth washload. Increase that to two loads when you've grown accustomed to the new detergent. The impact, if we all do that, is immense. We may even switch completely to phosphate-free laundry products.

Choices about environmentally conscious consuming are not a matter of all or nothing. Of course, the "greener" your household, the more you'll be helping to save the environment. But you need not feel guilty about making changes at a pace that suits your preferences and lifestyle.

When you first begin to use *The Green Pages*, target the areas of your household where you know you'll be comfortable making changes. Once an area of your house or room is up to the level you desire, move on to the next. Eventually, green shopping will become second nature to you. And we hope, as more manufacturers realize the economic benefit of selling environmentally responsible products, that we'll see a larger selection in the supermarket, drug store, and department store aisles. If you do have favorite products that are not acceptable from an environmental standpoint (excess packaging, unnecessary chemicals, etc.), write a letter to the manufacturer—if enough people raise their voices, the forces of the free market will cause companies to reformulate and repackage their goods. As the late Malcolm Forbes wrote in Forbes magazine, "If 90 percent of your customers paid you to package 'green,' wouldn't you be awfully stupid not to?"

Finally, if you learn of products that aren't listed in *The Green Pages*, drop us a note and we'll make an effort to include them in a future edition. We look forward to hearing from you because cleaning up the environment is partially about sharing information. No, we all won't improve the environment overnight by buying green and practicing good consuming behavior. But together, we can begin making a dent that will ultimately lead to a cleaner and safer environment for our children and grandchildren.

PART I

The Market Shopper's Guide

CHAPTER 1

The Laundry

N OBODY WANTS to go back to pounding dirty clothes on a flat rock on the river bank, but the modern American laundry room is not particularly kind to the environment. Every year, American households consume:

◆ One billion gallons of liquid detergent and bleach, enough to fill a lake 4 miles wide, 2 miles long, and 10 feet deep.

◆ Four billion pounds of laundry detergents, a little over 16 pounds per person.

◆ One trillion gallons of water, enough to fill a lake 400 hundred miles wide, 200 hundred miles long, and 10 feet deep.

The cardboard boxes and plastic bottles that detergents are packaged in wind up in landfills, which are rapidly nearing their ultimate capacity. The laundry detergents, bleaches, fabric softeners, spot removers, and other chemicals end up in overloaded sewage treatment facilities, and ultimately in our waterways.

☞ Detergents

Why don't we get rid of most of these problems by just going back to old-fashioned soap? Because if your water is not soft, soap will not do a very good job of cleaning your clothes, especially in cold water. In fact, if the water is hard—has a high mineral content—the soap will be deposited on the clothes, making them look even worse.

Detergents, generally made from petroleum products,

work much better because they are highly soluble in cold water and they don't leave deposits on clothes. Introduced in the 1950s, the first detergents were not biodegradable, with the result that large amounts of foam were spilled into rivers and lakes. And manufacturers initially used phosphates as "builders" to keep dirt from being redeposited on clothes. Phosphates are crucial nutrients for bacteria and algae; high quantities in waste water promotes their growth. When these microorganisms die, their decay uses up the oxygen in water, suffocating fish and other wildlife. Phosphates in sewage were a key factor in the "death" of Lake Erie in the 1960s.

But detergent manufacturers have cleaned up their act, so to speak. Some manufacturers have abandoned phosphates altogether, switching to less-effective builders. Almost all detergents sold in the U.S. are now biodegradable, either phosphate-free or low-phosphate.

Liquids versus Powders

Nearly half of all detergents now sold in the U.S. are liquids. They contain virtually the same ingredients as powders, but usually half as much liquid per washload is required. On the other hand, though, liquids come in plastic bottles, powders in cardboard boxes.

☞ Softeners

Fabric softeners are special detergents that prevent buildup of static electricity. Because they are biodegradable and contain no builders, they do not represent a serious pollution problem. Although present in very low concentrations, perfumes in fabric softeners and detergents are clearly unnecessary. Fabric softener "sheets" are preferable because they do not contribute to water pollution and are generally not packaged in plastic.

☞ Enzymes

Enzymes are an increasingly important component of laundry detergents. These proteins break down the chemicals that cause grass and food stains, among others, thereby making soaps and detergents more effective, especially in cold water. They minimize the need for other types of pre-washes. They are themselves biodegradable and do not pose a pollution problem.

Enzymes were very popular in detergents during the 1970s, but were removed from the market when it was discovered that workers in detergent and enzyme factories were developing allergic reactions. This problem was overcome by microencapsulating the enzymes in tiny spheres that dissolve in water. Now, more than half of all detergents sold in the U.S. contain enzymes.

☞ Bleaches

Liquid versus Powder

Chlorine bleaches are frequently used as disinfectants and stain-removers, particularly for white clothes. But chlorine is highly reactive and can combine with other elements in the environment to create toxic substances. Typically, however, bleach is diluted in sewers to very low concentrations.

Powdered bleaches usually contain chemicals that release a highly reactive form of oxygen that removes stains. These products do not have the characteristic odor of liquid bleaches, are safer for delicate and colored fabrics, and do not combine with other materials in waste water to form toxic compounds.

Overall, the advantage goes to powders, but if you must use chlorine bleach as a disinfectant, use as little as possible.

☞ **Green Thinking** _____

What You Can Do at Home

By taking a few simple steps, you can make a big difference to the environment when you do your laundry and save yourself some money at the same time.

DO:
✔ Use cold-water rinses always.

✔ Use cold water for the wash cycle as much as possible. As much as 90 percent of the energy used for washing clothes goes to heating water.

✔ Wash full loads rather than partial loads. You'll use less water; washing machines use thirty to sixty gallons of water for each cycle.

✔ Buy energy-efficient washers and dryers and water-efficient washers.

DON'T:
✘ Don't use the manufacturer's recommended amount of detergent. You can usually get your clothes clean with about half as much. Experiment until you find the best quantity.

✘ Don't use soap if you have hard water—it will ruin your clothes. If you are not sure, Culligan and other water-softener companies will test your water for you. If you have water that has some hardness, a little sodium bicarbonate added to the soap will act as a builder, minimizing the redeposit of dirt on the clothes.

✘ Don't be afraid to experiment. We list many multiple-purpose products in the "Broom Closet" chapter for use in laundering. These are often much better for the environment—and are among the best bargains available. Find what works best in your water.

☞ Anatomy of a Green Product

The key to buying environmentally sound laundry products is reading labels. Whenever possible, buy the largest package available; you'll save money and reduce the amount of packaging that must be disposed of. Detergents that come in individual packages, one per wash, should be avoided. Those that contain a fabric softener will reduce separate packaging waste if they work satisfactorily.

The most environmentally desirable products have the following characteristics:

Laundry Soaps and Detergents
100 percent natural (no synthetic chemicals, applies only to soaps), phosphate-free, chlorine-free, vegetable oil base, unscented, dye-free, concentrated, recycled and/or recyclable packaging.

Bleaches
Powdered, chlorine-free, concentrated, recycled and/or recyclable packaging.

Miscellaneous Laundry Products
Same criteria as other laundry products.

Product	Manufacturer	Description

Laundry Soaps and Detergents

Product	Manufacturer	Description
Allen's Naturally Laundry Detergent (Liquid)	Allen's Naturally	Phosphate-free Chlorine-free Unscented Dye-free Highly concentrated
Arm & Hammer Detergent (Powder)	Church & Dwight	Phosphate-free Chlorine-free Recycled packaging
Cheer-Free (Powder)	Proctor & Gamble	Phosphate-free Chlorine-free Unscented Dye-free Recycled packaging
Country Safe Laundry Detergent (Powder)	Country Safe Corp.	Phosphate-free Chlorine-free Concentrated
Ecover Laundry Powder (Powder)	Mercantile Food Co.	100% Natural Phosphate-free Chlorine-free Vegetable oil base
Ecover Liquid Laundry Soap (Liquid)	Mercantile Food Co.	100% Natural Phosphate-free Chlorine-free Vegetable oil base
Ivory Snow (Powder)	Proctor & Gamble	Phosphate-free Chlorine-free Recycled packaging
Life Tree Premium Laundry Soap (Liquid)	Sierra Dawn	Phosphate-free Chlorine-free Dye-free
Natural Castile Soap (Liquid)	Community Soap Factory	100% Natural Phosphate-free Chlorine-free Vegetable oil base Dye-free
President's Choice Laundry Detergent (Powder)	Loblaws International	Phosphate-free Chlorine-free Unscented

Product	Manufacturer	Description
Surf (Powder)	*Lever Bros.*	Phosphate-free Chlorine-free
Tide (Powder)	*Proctor & Gamble*	Chlorine-free Recycled packaging
Tide (Liquid)	*Proctor & Gamble*	Phosphate-free Chlorine-free
Tide Unscented (Powder)	*Proctor & Gamble*	Chlorine-free Unscented Recycled packaging
Winter White Laundry Powder (Powder)	*Mountain Fresh Products*	Phosphate-free Chlorine-free Concentrated
Winter White Laundry Soap (Liquid)	*Mountain Fresh Products*	Phosphate-free Chlorine-free Concentrated
Winter White Pre-Wash (Liquid)	*Mountain Fresh Products*	Chlorine-free Phosphate-free

Bleaches

Product	Manufacturer	Description
Arm & Hammer Washing Soda (Powder)	*Church & Dwight*	Chlorine-free Recycled packaging
Axion (Powder)	*Colgate-Palmolive*	Chlorine-free
Biz Bleach (Powder)	*Proctor & Gamble*	Chlorine-free
Borateem (Powder)	*Dial Corp.*	Chlorine-free
Borax (Powder)	*US Borax & Chemical Co.*	Chlorine-free
Bright Water All Fabric Bleach (Liquid)	*Kleen Brite Laboratories*	Chlorine-free
Clorox 2 (Powder)	*Clorox Co.*	Chlorine-free Recycled packaging
Snowy Bleach (Powder)	*Airwick Industries*	Chlorine-free

Product	Manufacturer	Description
Winter White Bleach (Liquid)	*Mountain Fresh Products*	Chlorine-free Concentrated

Miscellaneous Laundry Products

Product	Manufacturer	Description
Allen's Naturally Fabric Soft (Liquid)	*Allen's Naturally*	Phosphate-free Chlorine-free Unscented Dye-free Concentrated
Bounce Unscented Fabric Softener (Sheets)	*Proctor & Gamble*	Unscented
Ecover Fabric Conditioner (Liquid)	*Mercantile Food Co.*	100% Natural Phosphate-free Chlorine-free Vegetable oil base
Ecover Wool Wash (Liquid)	*Mercantile Food Co.*	100% Natural Phosphate-free Chlorine-free Vegetable oil base
Faultless Dry White Starch (Powder)	*Bon Ami/Faultless Starch Co.*	Biodegradable Phosphate-free Chlorine-free
Golden Lotus Soft-n-Fresh (Liquid)	*Mountain Fresh Products*	Phosphate-free Chlorine-free Concentrated
Woolite (Liquid)	*Boyle-Midway*	Phosphate-free Chlorine-free
Woolite (Powder)	*Boyle-Midway*	Phosphate-free Chlorine-free

CHAPTER 2

The Kitchen

T HE KITCHEN is responsible for the bulk of the packaging waste that comes into the home. Now that more families have two wage earners, heavily packaged single-serve and convenience foods have skyrocketed in popularity, causing the amount of trash generated in the average home to more than double in just 20 years. Some examples:

- One out of every $10 that Americans spend on food goes to packaging. According to the U.S. Department of Agriculture, the amount of money spent on packaging last year, $28 billion, was greater than the net income of all American farmers.

- About 50 percent of the paper used in the U.S., 90 percent of glass, and 11 percent of aluminum goes for packaging.

- We throw out enough aluminum from cans and food containers every three months to rebuild the entire American commercial jet aircraft fleet.

This abundance of packaging materials is doubly problematic. On the one hand, irreplaceable natural resources are being dug out of the ground and wasted at a rate that will deplete all of our supplies sometime in the next century. On the other hand, mountains of trash are being buried, using up precious space near cities and polluting water sources.

☞ Food

The contents of food are beyond the scope of this book. Similarly, it is not possible to name every single brand that is packaged responsibly. But some broad generalizations are possible. Overall, the fresher the food is and the fewer additives and contaminants it contains, the better it is for both your internal environment and the environment at large. And the less packaging that is used to get it to you, the better it is for the environment.

Breakfast

Milk in waxed cardboard containers is preferable to milk in plastic bottles because the cardboard has less of an impact on the environment. Unfortunately, many manufacturers are coating the cardboard with plastic instead of wax, making them impossible to recycle.

Cardboard milk containers were, in the past, found to contain highly toxic dioxins, which are formed during bleaching of the paper. The U.S. Food and Drug Administration (FDA) says that is no longer a problem, but some experts disagree and recommend that people buy milk in plastic containers.

Some plastic milk jugs are made with HDPE plastic, which is recyclable (see below), and are therefore the containers of choice if available.

- ◆ Eggs should be purchased in cardboard containers or recycled materials, not foam.

- ◆ Ideally, breakfast cereals should be packaged in recycled cardboard boxes. About half of all cardboard packages in supermarkets are now made from recycled paper; look for the label that says it's recycled.

- ◆ Buy unbleached paper filters for your coffeemaker or buy filters that are whitened with an oxygen bleach rather than a chlorine bleach (see product listings).

Lunch

- ◆ If you pack your lunch for school or work, avoid prepackaged meals that contain several small packages of cheese, crackers, meat, and so forth, each in its own plastic or foil wrapper. Such products represent a gross misuse of packaging, and are also expensive.

- ◆ Purchase lunch meats at the deli section of the supermarket and ask the clerk to wrap them in paper instead of heavy plastic. Store them in a tightly sealed container at home.

- ◆ Avoid individual servings of foods packed in plastic for use in the microwave.

- ◆ Reuse plastic grocery bags and other bags.

- ◆ If you pack a sandwich, wrap it in waxed paper or cellophane rather than plastic bags, or recycle bags you already have.

- ◆ If possible, purchase drinks in large recyclable cans and bottles. Prepackaged juices in individual -serving sizes are a waste of resources and contribute to landfill burden. Use a Thermos bottle whenever possible.

Dinner

- ◆ Avoid fruits and vegetables that are prepackaged in plastic containers. By selecting your own out of a bin you'll be better able to pick quality produce and will reduce unnecessary packaging. Urge your supermarket to provide food in bulk.

- ◆ If possible, shop at local farmers' markets for produce; there is less packaging and the produce is fresher.

- ◆ Whenever possible, purchase products like pasta in cardboard boxes rather than plastic containers or bags. Pasta packaged in cellophane is also excellent from an environmental standpoint. Unfortunately, it is often difficult to tell the difference between cellophane and polystyrene (see the packaging section below).

- If you are microwaving your dinner, it's better to use a glass bowl with a lid rather than plastic wrap to reduce spattering.

- Don't buy plastic squeeze bottles of ketchup and other foods. The bottles are made from layers of different plastics and thus cannot be recycled.

- Eat less meat. The production of 1 pound of beef, for example, requires 16 pounds of grain and soybeans and 2,500 gallons of water. Eating less meat would also reduce the need to import beef from Central and South America, where increasing cattle production has contributed significantly to deforestation. And, according to most medical sources, it would be better for your health.

Pesticides

Pesticide residues in fruit and vegetables represent a highly controversial and complex problem to which there are no easy answers. Modern agribusiness is based on the use of pesticides, herbicides, and synthetic fertilizers to maintain high levels of production. A growing number of experts believe that many farmers use too many and too much of these chemicals, which pollute our water supplies and leave residues on our food.

There is generally no agreement about the health effects of pesticide residues. Most environmental groups charge that they are a health risk, especially to children. Most government agencies assert that levels of pesticides in fruits and vegetables are so low that they pose no risk, even to children.

If you are concerned about pesticides on your fruits and vegetables, purchase foods grown organically, without any pesticides or chemicals. They generally cost more, but may in the long run prove healthier for you and your family. If you do not have access to organic foods, carefully wash produce with soap and water before cooking or eating it, and peel when you can, especially citrus fruits. This will help to remove potentially harmful chemicals. There is no need to buy products that are supposedly designed to clean off pesticides. Most tests show they don't do any better than regular soap.

Antibiotics in Meat

Low levels of antibiotics are routinely given to cattle and poultry. For reasons that are not entirely clear to biologists, antibiotics promote growth so that animals gain more weight over less time, conception rates and litter sizes increase, and chicken eggshells are strengthened.

Some scientists believe that this process contributes to the development of antibiotic resistance in bacteria. When bacteria develop resistance to a given antibiotic, more powerful antibiotics must be used to combat an infection; those more powerful antibiotics often have a greater risk of side effects. Antibiotic-resistant bacteria are, in fact, becoming more common in human populations.

Critics also charge that the antibiotic-resistant bacteria are transferred directly from animals to humans in meat and that these bacteria cause disease in humans. That claim has never been proven, however, and the FDA considers the practice safe. If you are concerned about the health risk from antibiotics in meat, look for meat packages whose labels state that the contents are antibiotic-free. These are becoming increasingly available in major supermarkets. If your favorite market does not purchase antibiotic-free meat, let the store's management know your preference.

☞ Baby Food

What kind of food should you feed your baby? Throughout history, babies have eaten the same foods that their parents ate with no ill effects. Only within the last half-century have we come to believe that they should have their own food, packaged in individual-serving sizes. And then we loaded it up with salt and other additives so that it tasted good to the mother, whether it was good for the infant or not.

Today, major baby-food manufacturers have changed their products. The foods do not contain nearly as much salt or other additives as they did just 10 years ago, and are generally better for the baby. But why go to that added expense, not to mention the disposal problems associated with all those little bottles and boxes. For a very modest price, you can buy a small grinder that will allow you to serve your infant the same thing you are eating. You'll save money, your baby will be healthy, and you'll help the environment. If you must buy baby food, try your best to recycle the bottles, or reuse them—they make marvelous containers for nails, screws, buttons, and other pesky household items.

☞ Cooking

Use energy wisely when you are cooking. Don't fill the teakettle completely full of water to heat up enough for one cup of tea; the energy used to heat up all the unused water will simply go to waste. Keep your burners, ovens, and pilot light clean so that they burn efficiently. If you are buying a new stove, gas is preferable to electricity because it uses energy more efficiently; as much as 10 to 15 percent of the energy used to produce electricity is lost during transmission from the power plant to your home, but virtually no gas is lost during transmission. Gas is also cheaper. Choose a stove (and a water heater, if you are buying a new one) that is electrically ignited, so you don't waste gas on the pilot.

Your Microwave

Your microwave is a very useful tool for cooking because it uses much less energy than a conventional stove, either electric or gas. It is also convenient for defrosting frozen foods, though it is best to allow such foods to defrost by themselves, either on the countertop or in the refrigerator, because that requires no energy.

Microwave radiation can cause cataracts and other disorders, but your oven should not be a cause for concern. Today's ovens are generally well built and shielded to prevent loss of microwave radiation. If you are concerned about radiation leakage, ask an appliance repairman to check it.

One aspect of your microwave that should concern you is the growing use of plastic packaging designed to brown and crisp foods or to pop corn. Special plastic devices that absorb radiation and heat have been approved by the FDA for use at temperatures up to about 300°F. But in the microwave they heat up to 500°F and higher, and at those temperatures some components of the plastic escape into the food. The presence of these materials has not yet been associated with a specific health hazard, but they are certainly not good for you. Instead of using such packaging, get a ceramic browning tray that will not contaminate food.

Early in 1990 researchers also reported that foods with a high salt content do not heat up well in microwaves. Apparently, the salt partially blocks the penetration of the microwaves, so that the middle of food does not get very warm even though the outside is burning. This can be a problem when heating up leftovers, because thorough heating is necessary to ensure that any bacteria are killed. Many processed foods of the type often sold for use in microwaves also contain high quantities of salt—another good reason not to buy them.

Barbecuing

For anyone who is concerned about carcinogens in food, barbecuing should be out of the question. When juice and grease drop onto hot coals or an electric element, organic chemicals they contain are converted into a broad variety of chemicals similar to those found in coal tar. Many of these migrate through the smoke back to the meat; this gives it the distinctive barbecued flavor. But many of these chemicals are well-known carcinogens, especially a family of compounds called polyaromatic hydrocarbons (PAH). No one has definitively proved that barbecuing causes cancer, but it is certainly something to be concerned about.

One possible solution to the PAH problem is a grill design in which the fat drips into a pan, rather than on the charcoal. These products expose far less of the food's surface area to any PAHs.

Another concern with barbecuing is its potential for air pollution. Charcoal lighter fluids are very volatile and much of what you pour on the charcoal evaporates. In the air, these hydrocarbons contribute to the formation of photochemical smog. California has announced plans to ban the use of charcoal lighter in the early 1990s because of its contribution to smog. A better alternative is to use an electric lighter, which releases no emissions. In the long run, it's also cheaper.

Think carefully about the utensils and dishes you use for cooking out and picnicking. Avoid plastic plates, saucers, and bowls, especially those made of foam. Use ceramic or China or heavy paper plates, which are biodegradable. The same is true for cups. Waxed paper cups are recyclable. If you must use plastic cups, take them home, wash them, and use them over and over again. Use your own silver or stainless steel utensils whenever possible. If there are occasions when you must use plastic forks and spoons, don't throw them away. They too can be taken home, washed, and reused.

☞ Packaging

Trash is becoming a crisis of unmanageable proportions in the U.S. An average-size American throws out the equivalent of his or her own weight in packaging every 30 days. By some estimates, that amount will almost double by the turn of the century. Packaging accounts for one-third of all municipal waste by weight, and as much as one-half by volume. If you minimize packaging, you'll also get more for your money.

Plastics

Plastics are a particular problem in landfills. Although they account for only about 7 percent of household trash by weight, they represent about 17 percent of trash added to landfills by volume. And unlike most other trash buried in dumps, plastic lasts forever. Less than 1 percent of plastic packaging is now recycled. But if the 20 billion plastic bottles and the 1 billion pounds of plastic trash bags currently used by Americans were recycled, our need for landfills would be reduced by 30 percent.

Look for unnecessary packaging and avoid it. For example, meat doesn't need to be packaged in a foam tray. Foam egg cartons are also unnecessary; cardboard cartons work just as well and are kinder to the environment.

"A Guide to Environmental Issues" at the end of this book describes the various types of plastic in use today. The chart in this section lists those plastics that are recyclable.

Biodegradable versus Conventional Plastics

So-called biodegradable plastics aren't an environmental bargain. Modern landfills are designed to keep out water, and under such conditions, biodegradable plastics will last nearly as long as regular ones. Most environmental groups now consider biodegradable plastics simply a marketing lure designed to seduce consumers into mistakenly thinking that they are helping the environment. Early in 1990 most manufacturers of trash bags began limiting their claims of biodegradability.

Biodegradable plastics are useful primarily for objects such as the plastic rings that hold soda cans and beer bottles together. Animals that swallow or get tangled in the can holders can die of choking or strangulation. A biodegradable can holder is effective as long as no animal happens upon it before it has fallen apart. Instead of switching to biodegradable plastics, it is far better to simply keep plastics out of landfills in the first place.

Cellophane

Cellophane is a substance made from wood pulp. It is biodegradable and therefore a good packaging choice from an environmental perspective. Many products these days are packaged in polystyrene, which looks and feels like cellophane. Polystyrene is made from petroleum products and is not biodegradable. Unfortunately, it is hard to distinguish the two without laboratory testing. If you hold a match to polystyrene it will melt, whereas cellophane will burst into flames. This is obviously not a practical test to conduct in the supermarket aisles. Besides, when you burn polystyrene, you set toxins loose into the atmosphere. Some producers are now using the symbol shown in the chart on page 19 to designate products packaged in cellophane.

Paper Goods

Whenever possible, you should use recycled rather than virgin paper. The reason is simple: recycling paper requires 60 percent less energy and 15 percent less water than producing virgin paper. It is also kinder to forests: recycling one ton of paper saves 17 trees. Many products packaged in recycled paper now bear the following symbol:

Bleached versus Unbleached Paper

Unbleached paper should always be purchased when available. The manufacture of white paper requires large amounts of chlorine bleach, which pollutes the waterways downstream of paper mills. It also leads to the production of dioxins, extremely toxic chemicals that can cause cancer and other diseases. Dioxins have been found at low levels in several bleached paper products, especially milk cartons and coffee filters. Unbleached coffee filters and other paper products are also becoming more widely available (see product listings).

Plastic versus Paper Grocery Bags

When the clerk at the supermarket asks you "Paper or plastic?" most people assume that the environmentally correct answer is paper. That is not necessarily correct. Some points to consider:

- ◆ Paper grocery bags do break down in landfills, but very slowly. Plastic bags, even biodegradable bags, will break down much more slowly in the landfill, but they will take up much less space while they are doing so.

- ◆ Paper grocery bags are made from virgin paper; recycled paper is simply not strong enough to hold the groceries without ripping.

- ◆ Plastic bags released into the environment are a hazard to both flora and fauna, especially near the seashore.

When you add up the pros and cons, the score is close. If your supermarket collects plastic or paper bags for reuse, then you are probably best off going with whatever reusable option is available. Of course, the best solution of all is not to use either paper or plastic. Buy large cloth or string bags to carry your groceries home in. They can be used over and over without harming the environment.

Kitchen Product Packaging

Packaging	Recycled	Recyclable	Comments
Cellophane	No	No	Biodegradable You may see the following symbol on packaging
Paper Egg Cartons	Yes	Yes	
Glass Bottles	Yes	Yes	
Aluminum Cans	Yes	Yes	
Polyethylene terephthalate (PET) Plastic	No	Yes	Look for recyling symbol on container
High-Density Polyethylene (HDPE) Plastic (milk, juice, and detergent jugs).	No	Yes	Look for recycling symbol on container
Paperboard–White	No	Yes	

Packaging	Recycled	Recyclable	Comments
Paperboard–Brown	Yes	Yes	
Tin Cans	No	Yes	
Squeezable Plastic Containers	No	No	Made from several types of plastics that cannot be separated during recyling.
Combination Plastic/Foil (example: juice boxes)	No	No	Components can't be separated during recycling.
Paper/Foil Containers (pet food pouches)	No	No	Components can't be separated during recycling.
"Waxed" Cardboard (example: milk and juice containers)	No	No	"Wax" is now HDPE plastic, and cannot be separated from cardboard for recycling.
Foam Egg Cartons	No	No	May contain CFCs

Recycling will undoubtedly prove to be the key to environmentally acceptable product packaging. But recycling options vary greatly from city to city. Hopefully, markets for recycled plastic products will develop, and this will provide an incentive for companies to establish recycling centers that can handle a broad spectrum of packaging materials. In the meantime, we recommend that you purchase products in glass and aluminum containers and take them to your local recycling center. Plastic bottles for soda containers are also acceptable in areas where there are appropriate recycling facilities.

☞ <u>Kitchen Cleaning</u>

Detergents

Dishwashing detergents for both manual and automatic dishwashing are similar to the detergents used for laundry, but they often have added scents. You should make sure to use a product that is low in phosphates or, better, phosphate-free. As an alternative to dishwashing liquids, use a liquid or powdered soap such as Ivory.

Oven Cleaners

Commercial oven cleaners are generally concentrated sodium or potassium hydroxide, also known as lye. This material is very caustic; it is hard on your oven and even harder on you. Particularly objectionable are spray oven cleaners; the propellants in them contribute to air pollution and smog formation, and the fine mist of caustic lye can damage your lungs.

☞ <u>Other Kitchen Products</u>

Non-stick sprays use hydrocarbon propellants, which contribute to air pollution and smog formation.

Synthetic plastic sponges will persist in landfills every bit as long as other forms of plastic. Use a natural sponge instead, or a washcloth.

☞ Green Thinking

What You Can Do at Home

With a determined effort, you can reduce the amount of trash you produce in your kitchen by two-thirds. And even if you are not firmly committed to such an effort, every bit you do will be a benefit to the environment, and often to your own pocketbook as well.

DO:

✔ Buy food and other products from the supermarket in the largest box or container that you can find. It saves packaging and saves you money. Use a smaller, refillable container for convenience and ease of handling.

✔ Use covered-glass food storage containers; don't cover bowls with plastic or aluminum foil.

✔ Buy waxed paper instead of plastic wrap. It is biodegradable.

✔ Recycle packaging as much as possible. Glass, many plastic bottles, aluminum cans, and tin cans are all recyclable.

✔ Recycle plastic bags yourself. Use plastic grocery bags to line your wastepaper basket, to carry your lunch in, and for similar tasks around the home. You can also take them back to the store and reuse them yourself.

✔ Avoid plastic foam packaging. Buy eggs, for example, in cardboard cartons, not foam containers. If you must buy foam egg containers, recycle them yourself. Use them for holding small objects, such as screws and nails, or donate them to day care centers for use in crafts.

✔ Buy unbleached paper items, such as coffee filters and paper towels, or products made with the oxygen bleaching process (see "A Guide to Environmental Issues" at the end of the book).

✔ Object to new disposable products before they become entrenched in the marketplace. Express your concern to the store manager, write the company that makes them, and, above all, don't buy them.

✔ Consider buying a trash compactor if your locality permits them. They are expensive, but they will reduce the volume of your trash by two-thirds to four-fifths.

DON'T:

✘ Don't use paper towels for routine purposes. Use cloth towels that can be washed and used over.

✘ Don't use disposable plates, cups, utensils, and napkins unless it is absolutely necessary. If you must use disposable dishes, use paper instead of plastic foam.

✘ Don't leave water running while you are washing dishes by hand. Turn on rinse water only when needed.

✘ Don't purchase foods sold in single-serving packages. They are very expensive and they invariably have much more packaging than is necessary.

✘ Don't use your microwave to defrost frozen food. Let it thaw out on the counter or in the refrigerator.

✘ Don't buy liquid soap in plastic bottles except in situations where you are concerned about bacterial transmission. Buy soap wrapped in paper.

✘ Don't buy aerosol sprays. Although they no longer contain the chlorofluorocarbons that damage the ozone layer, their hydrocarbon propellants contribute to smog and air pollution. Buy pump sprays instead.

☞ Anatomy of a Green Product

Whenever possible, buy the largest packages available or buy in bulk. Powders and solids packed in cardboard are preferable to those packed in plastic. Glass bottles are better than plastic, unless plastic is recycled in your area.

The following product listings contain a sampling of products packaged in recyclable or degradable packaging. Whenever possible, we have chosen items that are also a better nutritional value—that is, products that contain healthier (unsaturated) oils, additive-free, free of unnecessary chemicals, organically grown, and so on. In some cases, you will find only remarks concerning packaging. These products are minimally acceptable—that is, they are offered in preferable packaging but may not be free of unnecessary chemicals.

Again, it is beyond the scope of this book to recommend food products purely on the basis of health. If you have a special diet or certain goals regarding chemical reduction in your house and body, then apply the principles you've learned in this chapter to make purchasing decisions that suit your needs.

The most environmentally desirable products have the following characteristics:

Food Contents
Organic (pesticide-free), additive-free, preservative-free, no tropical oils, no or low sugar, recycled/recyclable/reusable packaging.

Paper Goods
100 percent recycled or natural fibers, biodegradable, dioxin-free (unbleached or oxygen-bleached), undyed, (or if dyed, then only light colors), unscented.

Cleaning Products
Biodegradable, phosphate-free, chlorine-free, vegetable oil base, unscented, dye-free, recycled and/or recyclable packaging.

Product	Manufacturer	Description

Kitchen Paper Products

Product	Manufacturer	Description
C.A.R.E. Coffee Filters (Paper)	Ashdun Industries	Recycled Biodegradable Unbleached
C.A.R.E. Napkins (Paper)	Ashdun Industries	Recycled Biodegradable Unbleached
C.A.R.E. Paper Towels (Paper)	Ashdun Industries	Recycled Biodegradable Unbleached
Chinet Bowls (Paper)	Keyes Fibre Co.	Biodegradable Recyclable
Eco-Filter Coffee Filter (Cotton)	Eco-Filter Products	100% Natural fiber Biodegradable Reusable/recyclable
Green Forest Paper Towels (Paper)	Fort Howard Corp.	Recycled Dye-free Unscented
Lola Bottle & Dish Brush (Vegetable Fiber/Wood)	Lola	100% Natural fiber Biodegradable Reusable/recyclable
Lunch Bags (Paper)	AJM Packaging	Biodegradable Recyclable
Melitta Coffee Filters (Paper)	Melitta North America	Biodegradable Available unbleached
Mr. Coffee Chlorine-Free Filter (Paper)	Mr. Coffee, Inc.	Dioxin-free paper
Natural Brew Coffee Filters (Paper)	Rockline, Inc.	Biodegradable Unbleached
Project Green Coffee Filters (Paper)	Shurfine-Central Corp.	Dioxin-free paper
Project Green Luncheon Napkins (Paper)	Shurfine-Central Corp.	Dioxin-free paper Dye-free Unscented
Project Green Paper Towels (Paper)	Shurfine-Central Corp.	Dioxin-free paper Dye-free Unscented

The Kitchen

Product	Manufacturer	Description
Save-a-Tree Shopping Bags (Cotton)	*Save-a-Tree*	100% Natural fiber Biodegradable Reusable
Servaides Napkins (Paper)	*Erving Paper Mills*	Dye-free
Swedish Chlorine Free Filters (Paper)	*Loblaw International Merchants*	Unbleached Biodegradable
Tree-Free Napkins	*Statler Tissue*	100% Recycled paper Dye-free Unscented
Tree-Free Paper Towels	*Statler Tissue*	100% Recycled paper Dye-free Unscented
Vegetable Fiber Scrub Brush (Vegetable Fiber)	*Kuroshio*	100% Natural fiber Biodegradable Reusable/recyclable
Waxtex Bags (Paper)	*Menominee Paper Co.*	Biodegradable
Waxtex Wrap (Paper)	*Menominee Paper Co.*	Biodegradable

Trash Bags

"Safe for the Environment" Glad Bags (Plastic)	*First Brands*	Partially recycled plastic

Kitchen Cleansers

Allen's Dish Soap (Liquid)	*Allen's Naturally*	Phosphate-free Chlorine-free Unscented Dye-free
Allen's Dishwasher Detergent (Powder)	*Allen's Naturally*	Chlorine-free Unscented Dye-free
Better Brew Coffee Maker Cleaner (Liquid)	*Twinoak Products*	Phosphate-free

Product	Manufacturer	Description
Brillo Copper Kit (No Soap Scouring Pad)	*Purex Corp.*	Phosphate-free
Chore Boy Copper Scouring Puff	*Airwick Industries*	Phosphate-free
Easy-Off Non-Caustic (Oven Clean/Liquid)	*Boyle-Midway*	Lye-free Odor-free
Ecover Dishwashing Soap (Liquid)	*Mercantile Food Co.*	100% Natural Biodegradable Phosphate-free Chlorine-free Vegetable oil base
Kleer Dish Detergent (Liquid)	*Mountain Fresh Products*	Phosphate-free Chlorine-free Dye-free Concentrated
Kleer II Dishwasher Gel (Liquid)	*Mountain Fresh Products*	Phosphate-free Concentrated
Kurly Kate Brass Pads	*Purex Corp.*	Phosphate-free
Life Tree Premium Dish Soap (Liquid)	*Sierra Dawn*	Phosphate-free Chlorine-free
Palmolive Dishwashing Soap (Liquid)	*Colgate-Palmolive*	Phosphate-free Chlorine-free
Supreme Steel Wool Pads	*Purex Corp.*	Phosphate-free

Cold Cereals

Amaranth Flakes Cereal	*Health Valley Foods*	Organic ingredients No artificial additives No preservatives Recyclable paperboard package
American Prairie Muesli (Wheat-Free)	*Mercantile Food Co.*	100% Organic ingredients No artificial additives No preservatives No oils Recyclable paperboard package

The
Kitchen

Product	Manufacturer	Description
American Prairie Muesli (Wheat-Free)	*Mercantile Food Co.*	100% Organic ingredients No artificial additives No preservatives No oils Recyclable paperboard package
Arrowhead Nature O's Cereal	*Arrowhead Mills, Inc.*	No artificial additives No preservatives No oils No sugar
Arrowhead Puffed Corn Cereal	*Arrowhead Mills, Inc.*	No artificial additives No preservatives No oils No sugar
Arrowhead Puffed Millet Cereal	*Arrowhead Mills, Inc.*	No artificial additives No preservatives No oils No sugar
Arrowhead Puffed Rice Cereal	*Arrowhead Mills, Inc.*	No artificial additives No preservatives No oils No sugar
Arrowhead Puffed Wheat Cereal	*Arrowhead Mills, Inc.*	No artificial additives No preservatives No oils No sugar
Barbara's Natural Cereals	*Barbara's Bakery*	No artificial additives No preservatives Recyclable paperboard package
Cheerios	*General Mills*	No artificial additives Low sugar Recycled paper Recyclable paperboard package
Corn Chex	*Ralston Purina*	No artificial additives Low sugar Recycled paper Recyclable paperboard package
Erewhon Crispy Brown Rice Cereal	*Erewhon/U.S. Mills*	Organic ingredients No artificial additives No preservatives Recycled paper Recyclable paperboard package

Product	Manufacturer	Description
Erewhon Fruit'n Wheat Cereal	Erewhon/U.S. Mills	Organic ingredients No artificial additives No preservatives Recycled paper Recyclable paperboard package
Erewhon Raisin Bran	Erewhon/U.S. Mills	Organic ingredients No artificial additives No preservatives Recycled paper Recyclable paperboard package
Erewhon Wheat Flakes	Erewhon/U.S. Mills	Organic ingredients No artificial additives No preservatives Recycled paper Recyclable paperboard package
Grape Nuts	General Foods	No artificial additives No preservatives No sugar Recycled paper Recyclable paperboard package
Health Valley Oat Bran Flakes	Health Valley Foods	No artificial additives No preservatives No oils No sugar Recyclable paperboard package
Health Valley Oat Bran O's	Health Valley Foods	No artificial additives No preservatives No oils No sugar Recyclable paperboard package
Health Valley Raisin Bran	Health Valley Foods	No artificial additives No preservatives No oils No sugar Recyclable paperboard package
Kellogg's Corn Flakes	Kellogg's	No artificial additives No preservatives Low sugar Recycled paper Recyclable paperboard package

The Kitchen

Product	Manufacturer	Description
Kretschmer Wheat Germ	*Quaker Oats Co.*	No artificial additives No preservatives No sugar Glass packaging
Maple Corns Cereal	*Arrowhead Mills, Inc.*	Organic ingredients No artificial additives No preservatives Recyclable paperboard package
New Morning Cereals	*New Morning*	Organic ingredients No artificial additives No preservatives Recyclable paperboard package
NutriGrain Corn	*Kellogg's*	No artificial additives No preservatives No sugar Recycled paper Recyclable paperboard package
NutriGrain Nuggets	*Kellogg's*	No artificial additives No preservatives No sugar Recycled paper Recyclable paperboard package
NutriGrain Wheat	*Kellogg's*	No artificial additives No preservatives No sugar Recycled paper Recyclable paperboard package
Product 19	*Kellogg's*	No preservatives Low sugar Recycled paper Recyclable paperboard package
Quaker Puffed Rice Cereal	*Quaker Oats Co.*	No artificial additives No preservatives No oils No sugar Recyclable paperboard package
Quaker Puffed Wheat Cereal	*Quaker Oats Co.*	No artificial additives No preservatives No oils No sugar Recyclable paperboard package

Product	Manufacturer	Description
Rice Chex	*Ralston Purina*	No artificial additives Low sugar Recycled paper Recyclable paperboard package
Rice Krispies	*Kellogg's*	No artificial additives Low sugar Recycled paper Recyclable paperboard package
Shredded Wheat	*R.J. Nabisco*	No artificial additives No sugar Recycled paper Recyclable paperboard packag
Shredded Wheat'n Bran	*R.J. Nabisco*	No artificial additives No sugar Recycled paper Recyclable paperboard package
Special K	*Kellogg's*	Low sugar Recycled paper Recyclable paperboard package
Sunshine Shredded Wheat	*Sunshine Biscuits, Inc.*	No Artificial additives No oils No sugar Recyclable paperboard package
Wheat Chex	*Ralston Purina*	No artificial additives Low sugar Recycled paper Recyclable paperboard package
Wheaties	*General Mills*	No artificial additives No preservatives Low sugar Recycled paper Recyclable paperboard package

Hot Cereals

Product	Manufacturer	Description
7 Grain Hot Cereal	*Arrowhead Mills, Inc.*	No artificial additives No preservatives No oils No sugar Recyclable paperboard package

Product	Manufacturer	Description
American Prairie 5-Grain Cereal	*Mercantile Food Co.*	100% Organic ingredients No artificial additives No preservatives No oils Recyclable paperboard package
American Prairie Maple Raisin	*Mercantile Food Co.*	100% Organic ingredients No artificial additives No preservatives No oils Recyclable paperboard package
American Prairie Maple Rye	*Mercantile Food Co.*	100% Organic ingredients No artificial additives No preservatives No oils Recyclable paperboard package
American Prairie Quick Oats	*Mercantile Food Co.*	100% Organic ingredients No artificial additives No preservatives No oils Recyclable paperboard package
American Prairie Rye & Rice	*Mercantile Food Co.*	100% Organic ingredients No artificial additives No preservatives No oils Recyclable paperboard package
Bear Mush Hot Cereal	*Arrowhead Mills, Inc.*	No artificial additives No preservatives No oils No sugar Recyclable paperboard package
Cream of Rice	*R.J. Nabisco*	No artificial additives No preservatives No sugar Recycled paper Recyclable paperboard package
Cream of Wheat	*R.J. Nabisco*	No artificial additives No preservatives No sugar Recycled paper Recyclable paperboard package

Product	Manufacturer	Description
Farina	*Pillsbury*	No artificial additives No preservatives No sugar Recyclable paper Recyclable paperboard package
Mother's Hot Barley Cereal	*Quaker Oats Co.*	No artificial additives No preservatives No sugar Recyclable paperboard package
Mother's Oat Bran Hot Cereal	*Quaker Oats Co.*	No artificial additives No preservatives No sugar Recyclable paperboard package
Mother's Whole Wheat Hot Cereal	*Quaker Oats Co.*	No artificial additives No preservatives No sugar Recyclable paperboard package
Quaker Oats Bran	*Quaker Oats Co.*	No artificial additives No preservatives No oils No sugar Recyclable paperboard package
Quaker Oats Oat Bran	*Quaker Oats Co.*	No artificial additives No preservatives No oils No sugar Recyclable paperboard package
Quaker Old Fashioned Oats	*Quaker Oats Co.*	No artificial additives No preservatives No sugar Recyclable paperboard package
Wheatena	*American Home Foods*	No artificial additives No preservatives No sugar Recyclable paperboard package

The Kitchen

Miscellaneous Breakfast Foods

Product	Manufacturer	Description
Little Bear Croissants	*Little Bear Organic Foods*	Organic ingredients No artificial additives No preservatives Recyclable paperboard packag

Product	Manufacturer	Description
Nature's Warehouse Pastry Pops	*Nature's Warehouse*	No artificial additives No preservatives Fruit-sweetened Recyclable paperboard package

Juices

Product	Manufacturer	Description
After the Fall Natural Juices (Liquid)	*After the Fall Products*	No artificial additives No preservatives Glass packaging
After the Fall Organic Juices (Liquid)	*After the Fall Products*	Organic ingredients No artificial additives No preservatives Glass packaging
Apple & Eve Apple Cranberry (Liquid)	*Apple & Eve, Inc.*	No artificial additives No preservatives No added sugar Glass packaging
Apple & Eve Apple Juice (Liquid)	*Apple & Eve, Inc.*	No artificial additives No preservatives No added sugar Glass packaging
Apple & Eve Natural Cranberry (Liquid)	*Apple & Eve, Inc.*	No artificial additives No preservatives No added sugar Glass packaging
Indian Summer Apple Juice (Liquid)	*Indian Summer, Inc.*	No artificial additives No preservatives Glass packaging
Mott's Natural Apple Juice	*Motts USA/Cadbury Schweppes*	No Artificial additives No preservatives Glass packaging
Ocean Spray 100% Grapefruit (Liquid)	*Ocean Spray*	No artificial additives No preservatives Glass packaging
Recharge Sports Drink	*R.W. Knudsen Family*	No artificial additives No preservatives Glass or aluminum packaging

Product	Manufacturer	Description
Santa Cruz Organic Juices (Liquid)	*Santa Cruz Naturals*	100% Organic ingredients No artificial additives No preservatives Glass packaging
Santa Cruz Organic Lemonade (Liquid)	*Santa Cruz Naturals*	100% Organic ingredients No artificial additives No preservatives Glass packaging
Sunsweet Prune Juice	*Sun-Dri Growers of CA*	No artificial additives No preservatives Glass packaging
Tropicana 100% Grapefruit (Liquid)	*Tropicana Products, Inc.*	No artificial additives No preservatives Glass packaging
Tropicana 100% Orange Juice (Liquid)	*Tropicana Products, Inc.*	No artificial additives No preservatives Glass packaging
Welch's 100% Grape Juice (Liquid)	*Welch's*	No artificial additives No preservatives Glass packaging

Snack Foods

American Natural Potato Chips	*American Natural Snacks*	100% Organic ingredients No artificial additives No preservatives Organic sunflower oil
Barbara's Corn Chips	*Barbara's Bakery*	No artificial additives No preservatives Safflower/sunflower oils
Barbara's Potato Chips	*Barbara's Bakery*	No artificial additives No preservatives Safflower/sunflower oils
Barbara's Whole Wheat Pretzels	*Barbara's Bakery*	No artificial additives No preservatives Safflower/sunflower oils

The Kitchen

Product	Manufacturer	Description
Bearitos Corn Chips	*Little Bear Organic Foods*	Organic ingredients No artificial additives No preservatives Corn oil
Cracker Jacks	*Borden, Inc.*	No artificial additives No preservatives Corn oil Recycled paper Recyclable paperboard package
Eagle Bavarian Hard Pretzels	*Eagle Snacks, Inc.*	No artificial additives No preservatives Recycled paper Recyclable paperboard package
Garden of Eatin Corn Chips	*Garden of Eatin, Inc.*	100% Organic ingredients No artificial additives No preservatives
Hain Rice Cakes	*Hain Pure Foods Co.*	No artificial additives No preservatives
Health Valley Cheddar Lites	*Health Valley Foods*	Organic corn No artificial additives No preservatives Safflower/sunflower oils
Health Valley Corn Chips	*Health Valley Foods*	No artificial additives No preservatives Safflower/sunflower oils
Little Bear Caramel Corn	*Little Bear Organic Foods*	Organic ingredients No artificial additives No preservatives Canola oil
Little Bear Flavored Popcorns	*Little Bear Organic Foods*	Organic ingredients No artificial additives No preservatives Safflower/canola oil
Little Bear Refried Beans	*Little Bear Organic Foods*	Organic ingredients No artificial additives No preservatives Safflower oil
Little Bear Taco Shells	*Little Bear Organic Foods*	Organic ingredients No artificial additives No preservatives Safflower oil

Product	Manufacturer	Description
Lundberg Organic Rice Cakes	*Lundberg Family Farms*	100% Organic ingredients No artificial additives No preservatives No oils
Lundberg Rice Cakes	*Lundberg Family Farms*	No artificial additives No preservatives No oils
Mister Salty Pretzels	*R.J. Nabisco*	No artificial additives No preservatives Recycled paper Recyclable paperboard package
Sun-Maid Raisins	*Sun-Growers of CA*	No artificial additives No preservatives Recyclable paperboard package

Crackers

Finn Crisp	*Shaffer, Clarke & Co.*	No artificial additives No preservatives No oils Recyclable paperboard package
Kavli Crispbread	*O. Kavli A/S*	No artificial additives No preservatives No oils Recyclable paperboard package
Lifestream Krispbreads	*Lifestream Natural Foods*	100% Organic ingredients No artificial additives No preservatives No oils Recycled paper Recyclable paperboard package
Manischewitz Whole Wheat Matzo	*Manischewitz*	No artificial additives No preservatives Recyclable paperboard package
Stoned Wheat Thins	*Christe Brown & Co.*	No artificial additives No preservatives Recyclable paperboard package

The Kitchen

Product	Manufacturer	Description
WASA Crispbread	*Wasabrod/Sandoz Nutritional Co*	No artificial additives No preservatives Soybean oil Paper packaging

Oils and Vinegars

Product	Manufacturer	Description
Bertolli Olive Oil (Liquid)	*Bertolli USA*	No artificial additives No preservatives Glass packaging
Cider Vinegar (Liquid)	*A.J. Heinz Co.*	No artificial additives No preservatives Glass packaging
Hain Pure Vegetable Oils (Liquid)	*Hain Pure Food Co.*	No artificial additives No preservatives Glass packaging
Mazola Corn Oil (Liquid)	*Best Foods*	No artificial additives No preservatives
Spectrum Naturals Olive Oil (Liquid)	*Spectrum Marketing, Inc.*	100% Organic ingredients No artificial additives No preservatives Glass packaging
Spectrum Naturals Safflower (Liquid)	*Spectrum Marketing, Inc.*	100% Organic ingredients No artificial additives No preservatives Glass packaging
Spectrum Naturals Sesame Oil (Liquid)	*Spectrum Marketing, Inc.*	100% Organic ingredients No artificial additives No preservatives Glass packaging
White Vinegar (Liquid)	*A.J. Heinz Co.*	No artificial additives No preservatives Glass packaging

Pasta and Sauces

Product	Manufacturer	Description
Buitoni Pastas	*Buitoni*	No artificial additives No preservatives Recycled paper Recyclable paperboard package

Product	Manufacturer	Description
De Boles Whole Wheat Pastas	*De Boles Nutritional Foods*	No artificial additives No preservatives Recyclable paperboard packag
Eden Flavored Pastas	*Eden Foods, Inc.*	Organic ingredients No artificial additives No preservatives
Enrico Organic Spaghetti Sauce (Liquid)	*Ventre Packing Co.*	Organic ingredients No artificial additives No preservatives Glass packaging
Enrico Spaghetti Sauce (Liquid)	*Ventre Packing Co.*	No artificial additives No preservatives Glass packaging
Hain Pasta & Sauce Meals	*Hain Pure Food Co.*	No artificial additives No preservatives Recyclable paperboard package
Macaroni & Cheese Dinners	*Fantastic Foods, Inc.*	Organic ingredients No artificial additives No preservatives No sugar Recyclable paperboard package
Muellers Pastas	*Best Foods*	No artificial additives No preservatives Recyclable paperboard package
Pasta Romana Pastas	*Buitoni*	No artificial additives No preservatives Recycled paper Recyclable paperboard package
Prince Pastas	*The Prince Co.*	No artificial additives No preservatives Recycled paper Recyclable paperboard package
Ronzoni Pastas	*Ronzoni*	No artificial additives No preservatives Recycled paper Recyclable paperboard package
Tree of Life Flavored Pastas	*Tree of Life Foods*	Organic ingredients No artificial additives No preservatives Recycled fiberboard tray

The Kitchen

CHAPTER 3

The Nursery

T HE MOST ENVIRONMENTALLY crucial decision you can make in the nursery involves the choice of whether to use disposable or cloth diapers.

- Americans throw away 18 billion diapers every year, enough to stretch to the moon and back seven times.

- It takes 36 million trees to produce this number of diapers.

- As much as 2 percent of the space in American landfills is taken up by disposable diapers, about one ton per year for each infant.

- About 2.8 million tons of untreated feces and urine end up in landfills rather than sewage each year because of the use of disposable diapers. This material contains pathogenic viruses and bacteria that can seep into the water supply.

- The use of disposable diapers for one child for 30 months (eight changes per day) costs $975, or about a dollar a day. Purchasing cloth diapers and washing them at home costs just $285 for the same period. Using cloth diapers and a diaper service costs from $10 to $15 a week, depending on where you live (this fee includes pickup and delivery).

☞ Diapers

Breaking the disposable diaper habit is a tough environmental issue. Polls show that as many as 87 percent of Americans prefer them for their convenience. But that convenience has a price: disposable diapers represent the largest single component in the waste stream after newspapers and beverage containers.

Diaper manufacturers have played on Americans' desire for convenience in the face of environmental problems by arguing that biodegradable diapers solve the problems associated with disposables. Such claims must be taken with a grain of salt. In a landfill, biodegradable diapers decompose in only a little less time than regular disposables, and some critics charge that they leave behind potentially hazardous residues.

In a controversial development in early 1990, an Arizona company announced plans to begin marketing a disposable plastic diaper that could be flushed down the toilet. This is possible, the company said, because the bikini-shaped diaper uses 40 percent less material than other disposables and it is lined with a plastic mixed with chalk. The chalk will break down in the acid normally found in sewage systems, the company said, breaking the plastic into small pieces. Sewage system operators, however, argue that the product will put extra strain on an already-overstressed system. Environmentalists agree, saying that the flushable diapers will simply convert a landfill problem into a water pollution problem.

Of course, there are some drawbacks to cloth diapers as well. Most people use large amounts of chlorine bleach to wash them at home. Home delivery service is expensive, and delivery trucks for diaper services pollute the air. Furthermore, many day-care centers and nurseries require that parents use disposable diapers. And, perhaps most important, disposables are simply more convenient; many people don't want to carry around dirty diapers.

Many parents of infants work full time, and washing diapers would be extremely inconvenient. Even a green consumer may be forced to use disposables, but using cloth diapers whenever it is feasible will make a dent in the diaper problem. That message seems to be getting across to consumers. The National Association of Diaper

Services reported a 39 percent increase in the number of customers using cloth diapers in 1989.

☞ Baby-Care Products

Talc

In the 1970s a small number of studies suggested that some types of talcum powder may contain asbestos, which causes lung disease and cancer. Follow-up studies, however, have failed to demonstrate such contamination, and the FDA says that commercial talcum powders are asbestos-free. But if you are still uncomfortable using talc to soothe baby's skin, try cornstarch instead or one of the commercial products that do not contain talc.

Nipples

In the mid-1970s, the FDA discovered that some nipples for baby bottles contained nitrosamines—potent carcinogens that can cause colon cancer—in concentrations as high as 350 parts per billion, well above the Federal limit of 10 parts per billion. The chemicals were a by-product of the manufacture of the synthetic rubbers used in the nipples.

Since then, manufacturers have revised their processes for making the nipples, and the FDA says the nitrosamine content of all nipples falls within the 10 parts per billion guideline. The content is so low that boiling will not remove any more of the chemical. If you are still uncomfortable with the idea of nitrosamines, alternative nipples made from silicone plastics are available. These contain no nitrosamines, but they are somewhat stiffer than regular nipples.

☞ Green Thinking

What You Can Do At Home

The recommendations for the nursery are short and simple.

DO:
Use cloth diapers whenever possible.

DON'T:
Don't use paper wipes to clean baby—use a washcloth instead.

☞ Anatomy of a Green Product

Choose products that are biodegradable and contain the fewest chemical additives. Recycled, recyclable, or reusable packaging is also important.

The most environmentally desirable products have the following characteristics:

Diapers
Multiple-use is best: natural fibers.
Single use: 100 percent biodegradable material.

Baby-care products
100 percent natural (no synthetic chemicals), biodegradable, vegetable oil base, talc-free, unscented, dye-free, recycled and/or recyclable packaging.

Nipples
Nitrosamine-free or low nitrosamine.

Bottles
Recyclable or reusable.

Note: You will not find many common baby-care products in the following listings because they often contain mineral oil, a petroleum-based substance, as well as dyes, fragrances, and other unnecessary substances. See Chapter 11 for a listing of mail-order baby-care products formulated with the environment in mind.

Product	Manufacturer	Description
Diapers		
Curity Diapers (Cotton)	*Curity*	Natural fiber Reusable/recyclable
Dappi Diaper Cover (Cotton Blend)	*TL Care*	Reusable/recyclable
Diaperaps Diaper Covers (Cotton Blend)	*Diaperaps*	Reusable/recyclable
Dovetails Diapers (Paper, Single-Use)	*Family Clubhouse*	100% Biodegradable Chemical-free Plastic-free Use with diaper cover
Nikky's Diaper Covers (Wool or Cotton)	*Nikky's*	Natural fiber Reusable/recyclable

The Nursery

Baby-Care Products

Product	Manufacturer	Description
Aubrey Natural Baby Bath Soap (Liquid)	*Aubrey Organics*	100% Natural Biodegradable Vegetable oil base
Aubrey Natural Baby Lotion (Liquid)	*Aubrey Organics*	100% Natural Biodegradable Vegetable oil base
Aubrey Natural Baby Shampoo (Liquid)	*Aubrey Organics*	100% Natural Biodegradable Vegetable oil base
Autumn Harp Extra Mild Baby Shampoo (Liquid)	*Autumn Harp, Inc.*	100% Natural Biodegradable Vegetable oil base
Baby Massage Baby Lotion (Liquid)	*Mountain Fresh Products*	Biodegradable Vegetable oil base Unscented Dye-free
Baby Massage Oil (Liquid)	*Mountain Fresh Products*	100% Natural Biodegradable Vegetable oil base Dye-free

Product	Manufacturer	Description
Baby Massage Tearless Shampoo (Liquid)	*Mountain Fresh Products*	Biodegradable Unscented Dye-free
Baby Massage Tearless Wash (Liquid)	*Mountain Fresh Products*	Biodegradable Unscented Dye-free
Baby Mild & Kind Child's Bath (Liquid)	*Borlind's of Germany*	Biodegradable Vegetable oil base
Baby Mild & Kind Shampoo (Liquid)	*Borlind's of Germany*	Biodegradable Vegetable oil base
Calendula Baby Cream (Cream)	*Weleda*	100% Natural Biodegradable Vegetable oil base
Calendula Baby Oil (Liquid)	*Weleda*	100% Natural Biodegradable Vegetable oil base
Calendula Baby Soap (Bar)	*Weleda*	100% Natural Biodegradable Vegetable oil base
Chicks Baby Lotion (Liquid)	*Jason Natural Products*	Biodegradable Vegetable oil base
Chicks Bubble Bath (Liquid)	*Jason Natural Products*	Biodegradable Vegetable oil base
Chicks Tearless Baby Shampoo (Liquid)	*Jason Natural Products*	Biodegradable Vegetable oil base
Cornstarch Baby Powder (Powder)	*Johnson & Johnson*	Biodegradable Talc-free Dye-free
Country Comfort Baby Cream (Cream)	*Country Comfort*	100% Natural Biodegradable Vegetable oil base
Country Comfort Baby Oil (Liquid)	*Country Comfort*	100% Natural Biodegradable Vegetable oil base
Country Comfort Baby Powder (Powder)	*Country Comfort*	100% Natural Biodegradable Talc-free

Product	Manufacturer	Description
Earthchild Baby Oil (Liquid)	Autumn Harp, Inc.	100% Natural Biodegradable Vegetable oil base
EcoLogical Baby Wipes (Paper)	Eco-Matrix	Biodegradable Dioxin-Free
Glass Baby Bottles (Glass)	Gerber Products	Biodegradable Recyclable/reusable
Glass Baby Bottles (Glass)	Even-Flo Products Co.	Biodegradable Recyclable/reusable
Lavender/Calendula Baby Oil (Liquid)	Lakon Herbals	Organic herbs and oils Biodegradable Vegetable oil base
Loanda Lavender Baby Soap (Bar)	Carme, Inc.	100% Natural Biodegradable Vegetable oil base
Natural Touch Diaper Wipes (Paper)	James River Corp.	Vegetable oil base
Nuk Nipples (Baby bottle nipples)	Gerber Products Company	Low-nitrosamine Reusable
President's Choice Green Moist Wipes (Baby wipes)	Loblaws International	Dioxin-free
Project Green Baby Wipes (Paper)	Shurfine-Central Corp.	Dioxin-free
Pur Nipples (Baby bottle nipples)	Infa/Monterey Labs	Nitrosamine-free Reusable
Rainwater Herbal Baby Shampoo (Liquid)	Nature's Gate/Levlad, Inc.	Biodegradable Vegetable oil base
Supermild Baby Castile Soap (Liquid)	All-One-God-Faith, Inc.	100% Natural Biodegradable Vegetable oil base
Talc-Free Baby Powder (Powder)	Autumn Harp, Inc.	100% Natural Biodegradable Talc-free
Teddy Baby Pacifier (Silicone)	American Baby Concepts	Nitrosamine-Free

The Nursery

Product	Manufacturer	Description
Tom's Honeysuckle Baby Shampoo (Liquid)	*Tom's of Maine*	100% Natural Biodegradable Vegetable oil base
Un-Petroleum Jelly (Cream)	*Autumn Harp, Inc.*	100% Natural Biodegradable Vegetable oil base
Vegelatum (Cream)	*Mountain Fresh Products*	Biodegradable Vegetable oil base Unscented Dye-free

CHAPTER 4

The Bathroom

C HANGING THE PRODUCTS you use in the bathroom can have a positive environmental impact:

- ◆ About 75 percent of the water usage in homes takes place in the bathroom.

- ◆ Brushing your teeth can use 10 gallons of water if you leave the faucet running; shaving can use 20.

- ◆ As much as a third of all water used in the home is simply flushed down the toilet. A leaky toilet can easily waste another 50 to 100 gallons of water per day.

- ◆ We use about 2 billion disposable razors every year. Because the metal blades can't easily be separated from the plastic, they are not recyclable.

- ◆ Plastic tampon applicators from sewage outfalls are one of the most common forms of trash on beaches. In some areas, they are now called "New Jersey seashells."

In addition to the problems of water use, overpackaging and overreliance on disposable products in the bathroom, inappropriate chemicals in cosmetics and other personal-care products are an important health as well as environmental consideration. Many cleaning agents used in the bathroom also present environmental risk. The green consumer can take certain simple steps to reduce environmental impact.

☞ General Considerations

Packaging is an important issue in the bathroom. Avoid products that have two or three layers of packaging when only one is necessary. Choose cardboard and paper packaging over plastic whenever possible. Manufacturers argue that plastic packaging is necessary to protect the purity of cosmetics and drugs, and especially for drugs, tamper-proof plastic packaging can provide a strong degree of confidence. But many first-aid products like bandages and sterile gauze have been packed in paper for years without any contamination problems.

Spray Cans

Aerosol products represent a particular problem in the bathroom— spray deodorants, hairsprays, and spray disinfectants, among others. Although none contain chlorofluorocarbons any longer, most use hydrocarbon propellants. Because these contribute to air pollution and smog, California plans to ban aerosol hairsprays and deodorants during the 1990s. Other cities and states are likely to follow suit. The fine drops produced by aerosol sprays are also easily inhaled and can end up lodged in your lungs. And finally, the empty spray cans represent a solid waste problem and a potential explosion hazard. For most products, there is no need for an aerosol; instead, you can use a pump or forms of the product that can be applied manually.

Petrochemicals

A broad variety of products ranging from shaving cream to mouthwash are made with petrochemicals. This practice is objectionable on several counts: for one, petrochemicals are a nonrenewable resource that should not be wasted frivolously. Their use also represents a risk to the environment in terms of air and water pollution.

But beyond these factors, petrochemicals pose a direct health hazard to the user. Formaldehyde, one of the most common ingredients, has irritating effects on the eyes, nose, and throat. Among the symptoms of poisoning by formaldehyde fumes are chronic eye irritations, respiratory problems, rashes, fatigue, confusion, and chronic thirst. Formaldehyde has also been linked to cancers of the sinuses, lung, and liver. Other petrochemicals have been linked to a variety of problems, including skin irritation, allergic reactions, and neurological damage.

The petrochemicals are often used as a base or emollient to help in the application or spread of various ingredients. Some are also used to keep major ingredients in solution. These functions can be filled by naturally occurring ingredients, which do not pose the same risks.

Colorings and dyes, usually made from petrochemicals, are another useless additive to most bathroom products, with certain obvious exceptions like nail polish and lipstick. Although they are usually present only in very small amounts, some of them have been associated with health risks, including cancer.

☞ Feminine Hygiene Products

Tampons and Napkins

Plastic tampon applicators are becoming one of the most common forms of trash on public beaches where they are washed up from sewage outfalls. In addition to being unsightly, they are often mistaken for food by birds and fish, who choke on them. Their use is unnecessary; cardboard applicators work just as well, and fall apart in the sewage system.

Biodegradable tampons and sanitary napkins are environmentally better than those that are not, but the improvement is modest because tampons are not likely to decompose in modern landfills. Recycled and unbleached fibers are preferable in tampons and sanitary napkins for the reasons given in the Paper Goods section, below.

☞ Shaving Products

Disposable razors are one of the most egregious wastes in the bathroom. Because the metal blade is encased in plastic, neither portion of the razor is recyclable. The ideal solution is to use an electric razor; you throw nothing away, and the amount of energy used by the electric razor is minuscule compared to that required to manufacture a disposable razor. Short of that, use a razor that has replaceable blades.

Avoid shaving creams containing formaldehyde and other petrochemicals. Aerosol cans also represent an unacceptable environmental risk, because of the propellants. Use shaving cream in a tube or an old-fashioned shaving brush and mug.

☞ Hair-Care Products

Shampoos and conditioners containing formaldehyde and other petrochemicals should be avoided. A variety of all-natural, effective ingredients is available. Aerosol hairsprays are unacceptable because of the hydrocarbon propellants, and the fine mist of the hairspray can be readily inhaled, with the potential to damage your lungs. If you want to use hair spray, use products with a pump spray. Although pumps use more plastic, they're better than aerosols from an air pollution and health standpoint. While mousse is available in spray form, tubes are kinder to the environment.

☞ Dental Products

Some brands of toothpaste and mouthwash contain formaldehyde or other petrochemicals. Avoid them. In fact, discuss with your dentist brushing with baking soda, at least some of the time (although the taste may not please you). If you are going to use toothpaste, buy it in a tube rather than in a pump, since tubes require less landfill space. Pumps waste plastic and take up too much space in a landfill.

☞ Deodorants

If—as not everyone does—you feel that you require a personal deodorant, use a stick or solid product, not a spray, and especially not an aerosol spray.

Room deodorants do not get rid of odors: they simply cover them with a stronger odor or anesthetize your nasal passages so you can't smell anything. If you have an odor problem in a room, open a window and let in fresh air. Try to find and eliminate the source of the odor by removing mildew and by cleaning areas that may be contaminated by odor-producing bacteria. Cleanliness is the best deodorant.

☞ Cosmetics

Cosmetics should, in general, contain no formaldehyde, petrochemicals, or unnecessary or artificial dyes or colorings. Natural products are available to take the place of all these materials, and a wide variety of all natural cosmetics are available.

The use of animals in testing cosmetics and other consumer products is an emotionally charged issue that is beyond the scope of this book. Animals have not been used in testing the cosmetics listed in this section, however.

☞ First-Aid Products and Drugs

The principal issue with first-aid products is packaging. Plastic and metal packaging should be avoided whenever possible in favor of cardboard and paper, which are adequate to maintain the sterility of most products. It must be recognized, however, that plastic packaging is important in some cases, particularly if a drug must be kept moisture-free or if a package must be tamper-proof. Even in these cases, choose the product that has the minimum necessary amount of packaging.

☞ **Personal-Care Products**

Most chemicals used with both soft and hard contact lenses are not an environmental problem. Chemical disinfection is carried out with a weak solution of hydrogen peroxide, which breaks down harmlessly to water and oxygen. And, for the most part, neither the saline solution used for rinsing nor the enzymes used for removing protein deposits are a problem. Some saline solutions and disinfectants, however, contain a small amount of thimerosal, which contains mercury. Mercury is a serious environmental pollutant; although present in very small amounts in disinfectants, every unnecessary use contributes to the environmental burden.

Talc

In 1976, researchers from the Mount Sinai Medical Center in New York reported that they had found asbestos fibers in some brands of talcum powder. It was believed that the asbestos came from nearby mines, but the FDA was never able to identify a source of contamination—nor was it able, in fact, to confirm that any talc had been contaminated with asbestos. Nonetheless, this chapter identifies products that are talc-free.

Cotton Products

Ideally, cotton balls should be packaged in paper, not plastic. Colored cotton balls should be avoided; the dyes are unnecessary. Cotton swabs should have a paper stick, not plastic.

☞ **Cleaning Products**

In general terms, the same consideration applies to bathroom cleaners as to those used in the kitchen.

Cleansers

Cleansers should be low-phosphate or phosphate-free. Most general purpose cleaners have ammonia and ethanol in them and, although ammonia is corrosive, neither one can be considered a severe pollutant. Bleaching cleaners contain hydrogen peroxide or sodium hypochlorite, the primary components found in powdered bleach. Neither of these is a severe pollutant. The two types should never be mixed, however, because they can produce dangerous fumes when combined. So read the labels carefully. In addition to ammonia, abrasive cleaners such as scouring powder contain trisodium phosphate, which contributes to the growth of algae in waterways.

Disinfectants

Disinfectants and mildew removers may contain hydrogen peroxide, the same chemical found in powdered bleach. To kill microorganisms, they release free oxygen atoms, which irritate skin though are not a serious pollution problem. Other disinfectants contain the much more toxic phenols. Again, watch for them on labels.

Toilet Cleaners

Toilet bowl cleaners typically contain hydrochloric acid or calcium hypochlorite, neither of which is a severe pollution problem. Some also contain paradichlorobenzene, which is toxic and a pollutant. Read the labels.

☞ Paper Goods

Paper products for use in the bathroom, as elsewhere, should be unbleached, or manufactured with an oxygen-bleaching process. Chlorine bleaching, used to whiten paper, is very detrimental to the environment, both because of the chemicals used and the production of dioxin contaminants during the bleaching process. These contaminants, which cause a variety of health problems (see the "Guide to Environmental Issues"), have been found in some bleached paper products.

Virgin versus Recycled

Whenever possible, use recycled paper products, even toilet tissue. It requires 60 percent less electricity and 15 percent less water to make recycled paper than to make virgin paper and, of course, recycling paper does not use any trees. In most cases, recycled paper is slightly less strong but in situations where that doesn't matter, it's preferable.

☞ __Green Thinking__ _____

What You Can Do at Home

You can save a lot of water in the bathroom, cut down on pollutants entering the water supply, and reduce packaging waste.

DO:

✔ Check your toilets for leaks. Put a little food coloring in the tank; if it appears in the bowl before you flush it, you've got a leak.

✔ Take short showers. Three to five gallons of water are washing down the drain each minute the shower is running, and you've paid to heat that water.

✔ Take a shower instead of a bath. It can use only one-third as much water.

✔ Install a flow-restricting shower head. Aerating heads make the pressure just as high as normal, but reduce the flow rate by almost half.

✔ Place a plastic bottle or bag, a water dam, or even a couple of bricks in your toilet tanks to reduce the amount of water wasted with each flush.

DON'T:

✗ Don't use disposable razors. Get a good metal razor in which you change the blade as needed. Better yet, use an electric razor.

✗ Don't leave the water running while you are shaving or brushing your teeth. Turn it on only when you need it. Don't use aerosol sprays. Try a pump spray alternative or use an alternative that doesn't require spray at all.

✗ Don't purchase tampons with plastic applicators.

✗ Don't throw used hypodermic needles (for injecting insulin, for example) in the trash. Ask your supplier for proper disposal practices in your area.

☞ Anatomy of a Green Product

Buy shampoo, conditioner, and other products in the largest packages possible; transfer to smaller containers for convenience. Choose glass bottles instead of plastic (and recycle or reuse them).

The most environmentally desirable products have the following characteristics:

Paper Goods
Recycled or natural fibers, biodegradable, dioxin-free (unbleached or oxygen-bleached), undyed (or if dyed, only light colors or prints), unscented.

Soaps, Dental Products, Body and Skin, Hair Care, Sun-Tanning Products, Deodorants, Shaving Products
100 percent natural (no synthetic chemicals), biodegradable, vegetable oil based, talc-free (body powders), unscented, dye-free, non-aerosol, recycled, recyclable, or reusable packaging.

Feminine Hygiene and Cosmetics
100 percent natural (no synthetic chemicals), biodegradable, vegetable oil base, unscented, dye-free. Tampons: applicator-free or biodegradable applicator, unscented.

Note: You may not find your favorite personal-care products in the following listings because they contain environmentally undesirable or unhealthy chemicals. For example, some soaps and deodorants contain formaldehyde, preservatives, dyes, fragrances, and bactericides. Some mouthwashes and toothpastes contain formaldehyde and dyes, as well as artificial sweeteners. Many personal-care products are also mineral-oil based. Chapter 12 contains a broad assortment of environmentally-friendly products that can be purchased through mail-order catalogs.

Product	Manufacturer	Description

Bathroom Paper Products

Product	Manufacturer	Description
C.A.R.E. Cotton Balls (Cotton)	*Ashdun Industries*	Recycled Natural fiber Biodegradable Unbleached
C.A.R.E. Cotton Swabs (Cotton)	*Ashdun Industries*	Recycled Natural fiber Biodegradable Unbleached
C.A.R.E. Facial Tissue (Paper)	*Ashdun Industries*	Recycled Biodegradable Unbleached
C.A.R.E. Toilet Paper (Paper)	*Ashdun Industries*	Recycled Biodegradable Unbleached
Charmin Free (Paper)	*Proctor & Gamble*	Biodegradable Unscented Dye-free
Chiffon Unscented (Paper)	*Crown Zellerbach*	Biodegradable Unscented
Cotton Balls (Paper)	*Johnson & Johnson*	Natural fiber Biodegradable Unscented Dye-free Paper packaging
Curity 100% Cotton Gauze Pads (Cotton)	*Colgate-Palmolive*	Natural fiber Biodegradable Unscented Dye-free
Curity Cotton Balls (Cotton)	*Colgate-Palmolive*	Natural fiber Biodegradable Unscented Dye-free Paper packaging
Envision Facial Tissues (Paper)	*Fort Howard Corp.*	Recycled Dye-free Unscented

Product	Manufacturer	Description
Envision Toilet Paper (Paper)	*Fort Howard Corp.*	Unbleached paper Recycled Dye-free Unscented Paper packaging
First Aid Paper Tape (Paper)	*Johnson & Johnson*	Biodegradable Dye-free Unscented
First Aid Rayon Tape (Paper)	*Johnson & Johnson*	Biodegradable Dye-free Unscented
Green Forest Toilet Paper (Paper)	*Fort Howard Corp.*	Recycled Dye-free Unscented
Johnson & Johnson Gauze Pads (Cotton)	*Johnson & Johnson*	Natural fiber Biodegradable Dye-free Unscented
K-Mart Quilted Squares (Cotton)	*K-Mart*	Natural fiber Biodegradable Dye-free Unscented
President's Choice Bathroom Tissue (Paper)	*Loblaws International*	Recycled paper Biodegradable
Project Green Facial Tissues (Paper)	*Shurfine-Central Corp.*	Dioxin-free paper Dye-free Unscented
Project Green Swabs (Paper)	*Shurfine-Central Corp.*	Dioxin-free paper Dye-free Unscented
Project Green Toilet Paper (Paper)	*Shurfine-Central Corp.*	Dioxin-free paper Dye-free Unscented
Q-Tips Cotton Balls (Cotton)	*Cheeseborough Ponds*	Natural fiber Biodegradable Dye-free Unscented
Scottissues (Paper)	*Scott*	Unscented

The Bath-room

Product	Manufacturer	Description
Tagsons Bathroom Tissue (Paper)	*Tagsons Papers, Inc.*	Recycled Biodegradable Dye-free Unscented
Tree-Free Toilet Paper	*Statler Tissue*	100% Recycled paper Dye-free Unscented

Soaps

Product	Manufacturer	Description
Alexandra Avery Soaps (Bar)	*Alexandra Avery*	100% Natural Biodegradable Vegetable oil base
Aubrey Soaps (Bar)	*Aubrey Organics*	100% Natural Biodegradable Vegetable oil base
Chandrika Ayurvedic Soap (Bar)	*Auromere*	100% Natural Biodegradable Vegetable oil base
Clearly Natural Glycerine Soap (Bar)	*Clearly Natural*	Biodegradable Vegetable oil base Unscented/scented
Dr. Bronner's Bar Soaps (Bar)	*All-One-God-Faith, Inc.*	100% Natural Biodegradable Vegetable oil base Dye-free
Dr. Bronner's Castile Soaps (Liquid)	*All-One-God-Faith, Inc.*	100% Natural Biodegradable Vegetable oil base Dye-free
Golden Lotus Soaps (Liquid)	*Mountain Fresh Products*	Biodegradable Vegetable oil base
Ivory (Bar)	*Proctor & Gamble*	Biodegradable
Jason Natural Soaps (Liquid)	*Jason Natural Products*	Biodegradable Vegetable oil base
Kirk's Coco Castile Soap (Bar)	*Proctor & Gamble*	Biodegradable Vegetable oil base

Product	Manufacturer	Description
Kiss My Face Olive Oil Soap (Bar)	Kiss My Face Corp.	100% Natural Biodegradable Vegetable oil base
Kiss My Face Pure Olive Oil Soap (Bar)	Kiss My Face Corp.	100% Natural Biodegradable Vegetable oil base Unscented
Naturade Aloe Vera 80 Soap (Liquid)	Naturade Products	Biodegradable Vegetable oil base
Natural Castile Soaps (Liquid)	Community Soap Factory	100% Natural Biodegradable Vegetable oil base
Nature de France Soaps (Bar)	Nature de France, Inc.	100% Natural Biodegradable Vegetable oil base
Orjene Soaps (Bar)	Orjene Natural Cosmetics	Biodegradable Vegetable oil base
Rokeach Coconut Oil Soap (Bar)	Rokeach & Sons	100% Natural Biodegradable Vegetable oil base
Sappo Hill Soaps (Bar)	Sappo Hill Soapworks	100% Natural Biodegradable Vegetable oil base Available in dye-free Available unscented
Sirena Soap (Liquid)	Sirena Products	Biodegradable Vegetable oil base Unscented Dye-free
Weleda Soaps (Bar)	Weleda	100% Natural Biodegradable Vegetable oil base

The Bath-room

Dental Products

Dentie Toothpaste (Paste)	Muso Co., Ltd.	100% Natural Biodegradable Vegetable oil base

Product	Manufacturer	Description
Homeodent Toothpaste (Paste)	*Boiron/Borneman, Inc.*	Biodegradable Vegetable oil base Dye-free
IPSAB Herbal Gum Treatment (Powder)	*Heritage Products*	100% Natural Biodegradable
IPSAB Tooth Powder (Powder)	*Heritage Products*	100% Natural Biodegradable
Ipsadent Herbal Mouthwash (Liquid)	*Heritage Products*	100% Natural Biodegradable Vegetable oil base
Mer-Flu-an Tooth Powder (Powder)	*American Merfluan, Inc.*	100% Natural Biodegradable
Natural Gum Toothpaste (Paste)	*Desert Essence*	Biodegradable Vegetable oil base Dye-free
Natural Mint Mouthwash (Liquid)	*Aubrey Organics*	100% Natural Biodegradable Vegetable oil base
Nature de France Toothpaste (Paste)	*Nature de France, Inc.*	100% Natural Biodegradable Vegetable oil base
Nature's Gate Mouthwashes (Liquid)	*Nature's Gate/Levlad, Inc.*	Biodegradable Vegetable oil base
Nature's Gate Toothpastes (Paste)	*Nature's Gate/Levlad, Inc.*	Biodegradable Vegetable oil base
Peelu Tooth Powder (Powder)	*Peelu Products*	Biodegradable Dye-free
Peelu Toothpaste (Paste)	*Peelu Products*	Biodegradable Vegetable oil base Dye-free
Rainbow Natural Mint Toothpast (Paste)	*Rainbow Research Corp.*	Biodegradable Vegetable oil base Dye-free
Tom's Natural Flossing Ribbon	*Tom's of Maine*	Recycled paper package

Product	Manufacturer	Description
Tom's Natural Mouthwash (Liquid)	*Tom's of Maine*	100% Natural Biodegradable Vegetable oil base
Tom's Natural Toothpastes (Paste)	*Tom's of Maine*	100% Natural Biodegradable Vegetable oil base Recycled paper Recyclable aluminum tube
Vicco Herbal Toothpaste (Paste)	*Auromere*	Biodegradable Vegetable oil base
Weleda Mouthwash Concentrate (Liquid)	*Weleda*	100% Natural Biodegradable Concentrated
Weleda Toothpastes (Paste)	*Weleda*	100% Natural Biodegradable Vegetable oil base

The Bath-room

Body and Skin Products

Product	Manufacturer	Description
Alba Botanica Lotions (Liquid)	*Alba Botanica Cosmetics*	Biodegradable Vegetable oil base
Alexandra Avery Creams (Liquid)	*Alexandra Avery*	Biodegradable Vegetable oil base
Alexandra Avery Lip Balms (Cream)	*Alexandra Avery*	Biodegradable Vegetable oil base
Aloegen Skin Emulsions (Liquid)	*Aloegen Natural Products*	Biodegradable Vegetable oil base
Amazing Grains Cleanser (Powder)	*Body Love Natural Cosmetics*	100% Natural Biodegradable Dye-free Concentrated
Analgesic Achillea Liniment (Liquid)	*Lakon Herbals*	Organic herbs and oils Biodegradable Vegetable oil base Glass packaging
Aqualin Oil Free Moisturizer (Liquid)	*Hlavin Cosmetics*	100% Natural Biodegradable

Product	Manufacturer	Description
Aubrey Facial Products (Liquid)	*Aubrey Organics*	100% Natural Biodegradable Vegetable oil base
Aubrey Moisterizers & Creams (Liquid)	*Aubrey Organics*	100% Natural Biodegradable Vegetable oil base
Aura Cacia Body Powders (Powder)	*Aura Cacia, Inc.*	100% Natural Biodegradable Talc-free
Autumn Harp Aloe Rose Body Lot (Liquid)	*Autumn Harp, Inc.*	100% Natural Biodegradable Vegetable oil base
Cleansing Milks (Liquid)	*Paul Penders Products*	Biodegradable Vegetable oil base
Cloudworks Rose Cream (Cream)	*Cloudworks, Inc.*	100% Natural Biodegradable Vegetable oil base
Comfrey Herbal Salve (Cream)	*Lakon Herbals*	Organic herbs and oils Biodegradable Vegetable oil base
Green Gold Herbal Salve (Cream)	*Cloudworks, Inc.*	100% Natural Biodegradable Vegetable oil base Dye-free
Jason Natural Body Lotions (Liquid)	*Jason Natural Products*	Biodegradable Vegetable oil base
Kiss My Face Moisturizers (Liquid)	*Kiss My Face Corp.*	Biodegradable Vegetable oil base
Monoi Bath & Shower Gel (Liquid)	*Monoi, Inc.*	100% Natural Biodegradable Vegetable oil base
Monoi Moisturizing Fluid (Liquid)	*Monoi, Inc.*	100% Natural Biodegradable Vegetable oil base
Moonsilk Body Powder (Powder)	*Alexandra Avery*	100% Natural Biodegradable Talc-free

Product	Manufacturer	Description
Naturade Aloe 80 Bubble Bath (Liquid)	*Naturade Products*	Biodegradable Vegetable oil base
Nature de France Clay Masks (Liquid)	*Nature de France, Inc.*	100% Natural Biodegradable
Nature's Gate Facial Products (Liquid)	*Nature's Gate/Levlad, Inc.*	Biodegradable Vegetable oil base
Orjene Cleansers (Liquid)	*Orjene Natural Cosmetics*	Biodegradable Vegetable oil base
Orjene Moisturizers (Liquid)	*Orjene Natural Cosmetics*	Biodegradable Vegetable oil base
Paul Penders Creams & Lotions (Cream)	*Paul Penders Products*	Biodegradable Vegetable oil base
Rainbow Golden Moisture Cream (Cream)	*Rainbow Research Corp.*	Biodegradable Vegetable oil base
Sombra Facial Scrubs & Masks (Cream)	*Sombra Cosmetics, Inc.*	Biodegradable Vegetable oil base
Soothing Herbal Blemish Treatment (Liquid)	*Lakon Herbals*	Organic herbs and oils Biodegradable Vegetable oil base Glass packaging
Terra Flora Body Powder (Powder)	*Terra Flora, Inc.*	100% Natural Biodegradable Talc-free
Weleda Lotions & Creams (Liquid)	*Weleda*	100% Natural Biodegradable Vegetable oil base

Hair-Care Products

Product	Manufacturer	Description
Aloegen Hair Spray (Liquid)	*Aloegen Natural Products*	Biodegradable Vegetable oil base
Aubrey Hair Conditioners (Liquid)	*Aubrey Organics*	100% Natural Biodegradable Vegetable oil base

The Bath-room

Product	Manufacturer	Description
Aubrey Hair Highliter Mousses (Liquid)	*Aubrey Organics*	100% Natural Biodegradable Vegetable oil base
Aubrey Herbal Shampoos (Liquid)	*Aubrey Organics*	100% Natural Biodegradable Vegetable oil base
Biogenic Conditioners (Liquid)	*Aloegen Natural Products*	Biodegradable Vegetable oil base
Biogenic Treatment Shampoo (Liquid)	*Aloegen Natural Products*	Biodegradable Vegetable oil base
Dr. Hauschka Neem Hair Lotion (Liquid)	*Dr. Hauschka Cosmetics, Inc.*	100% Natural Biodegradable Vegetable oil base
Golden Lotus Hair Conditioners (Liquid)	*Mountain Fresh Products*	Biodegradable Vegetable oil base
Golden Lotus Shampoos (Liquid)	*Mountain Fresh Products*	Biodegradable Vegetable oil base
Herbal Shampoos (Liquid)	*Community Soap Factory*	Biodegradable Vegetable oil base
J.R. Liggett's Bar Shampoo (Bar)	*J.R. Liggett, Ltd.*	100% Natural Biodegradable Vegetable oil base Concentrated Recyclable paper packaging
Jason Natural Conditioners (Liquid)	*Jason Natural Products*	Biodegradable Vegetable oil base
Jason Natural Shampoos (Liquid)	*Jason Natural Products*	Biodegradable Vegetable oil base
Kiss My Face Shampoos (Liquid)	*Kiss My Face Corp.*	Biodegradable Vegetable oil base
Light Touch Henna (Powder)	*Lotus Light, Inc.*	100% Natural Biodegradable
Natural Hairsprays (Liquid)	*Aubrey Organics*	100% Natural Biodegradable Vegetable oil base
Orjene Shampoos (Liquid)	*Orjene Natural Cosmetics*	Biodegradable Vegetable oil base

Product	Manufacturer	Description
Rainbow Henna (Powder)	*Rainbow Research Corp.*	Biodegradable Vegetable oil base
Rainbow Henna Conditioner (Liquid)	*Rainbow Research Corp.*	Biodegradable Vegetable oil base
Rainbow Henna Shampoo (Liquid)	*Rainbow Research Corp.*	Biodegradable Vegetable oil base
Rainwater Hair Conditioners (Liquid)	*Nature's Gate/Levlad, Inc.*	Biodegradable Vegetable oil base
Rainwater Herbal Shampoos (Liquid)	*Nature's Gate/Levlad, Inc.*	Biodegradable Vegetable oil base
VitaWave Hair Perms (Liquid)	*VitaWave Products*	100% Natural Biodegradable Vegetable oil base
Weleda Hair Conditioners (Liquid)	*Weleda*	100% Natural Biodegradable Vegetable oil base
Weleda Shampoos (Liquid)	*Weleda*	100% Natural Biodegradable Vegetable oil base Concentrated

The Bathroom

Sun-Tanning Products

Product	Manufacturer	Description
Aloe Gardenia Sun Oil (Liquid)	*Alexandra Avery*	100% Natural Biodegradable Vegetable oil base
Aura Cacia Sun Butter (Cream)	*Aura Cacia, Inc.*	100% Natural Biodegradable Vegetable oil base
Jason Sunbrellas Sunblock (Liquid)	*Jason Natural Products*	Biodegradable Vegetable oil base
Nature Tan SPF 4 & 8 (Liquid)	*Aubrey Organics*	100% Natural Biodegradable Vegetable oil base
Orjene Tanning Lotions (Liquid)	*Orjene Natural Cosmetics*	Biodegradable Vegetable oil base

Product	Manufacturer	Description
Rainbow Sunscreen Lotion (Liquid)	*Rainbow Research Corp.*	Biodegradable Vegetable oil base
Sunshade 15 Sunblock (Liquid)	*Aubrey Organics*	100% Natural Biodegradable Vegetable oil base

Deodorants

Product	Manufacturer	Description
Aubrey Natural Deodorants (Liquid)	*Aubrey Organics*	100% Natural Biodegradable Vegetable oil base Pump spray/CFC-free
Nature de France Deodorants (Stick)	*Nature de France, Inc.*	Biodegradable
Nature's Gate Roll-On Deodorants (Liquid)	*Nature's Gate/Levlad, Inc.*	Biodegradable Vegetable oil base
Orjene Stick Deodorants (Stick)	*Orjene Natural Cosmetics*	Biodegradable Vegetable oil base
Paul Penders Deodorant (Liquid)	*Paul Penders Products*	Biodegradable Vegetable oil base
Tom's Roll-On Anti-Perspirants (Liquid)	*Tom's of Maine*	Biodegradable Vegetable oil base
Tom's Roll-On/Stick Deodorants (Stick)	*Tom's of Maine*	Biodegradable Vegetable oil base
Weleda Sage Deodorant (Liquid)	*Weleda*	100% Natural Biodegradable Vegetable oil base Pump spray/CFC-free

Product	Manufacturer	Description

Shaving Products

Product	Manufacturer	Description
Alba After Shave Balm & Splash (Liquid)	*Alba Botanica Cosmetics*	Biodegradable Vegetable oil base
Alba Botanica Cream Shave (Cream)	*Alba Botanica Cosmetics*	Biodegradable Vegetable oil base
Ginseng Mint Aftershave (Liquid)	*Aubrey Organics*	100% Natural Biodegradable Vegetable oil base
Mint & Ginseng Shaving Cream (Cream)	*Aubrey Organics*	100% Natural Biodegradable Vegetable oil base
Penders After Shave Lotion (Liquid)	*Paul Penders Products*	Biodegradable Vegetable oil base
Tom's Shaving Creams (Cream)	*Tom's of Maine*	100% Natural Biodegradable Vegetable oil base Recycled paper Recyclable aluminum tube

The Bath-room

Feminine Hygiene and Cosmetics

Product	Manufacturer	Description
Alexandra Avery Perfumes (Liquid)	*Alexandra Avery*	100% Natural Biodegradable
Aubrey Eau de Colognes (Liquid)	*Aubrey Organics*	100% Natural Biodegradable Vegetable oil base
Aura Cacia Perfume Oils (Liquid)	*Aura Cacia, Inc.*	100% Natural Biodegradable Vegetable oil base
Bee Kind Natural Douche (Liquid)	*Bee Kind Products*	100% Natural Biodegradable Unscented Dye-free
Bio-Botanica Herbal Douche (Liquid)	*Bio-Botanica, Inc.*	100% Natural Biodegradable Dye-free Concentrated

Product	Manufacturer	Description
Cycles Mentrual Pads (Cotton)	Sisterly Works	100% Natural fibers Biodegradable Unscented Recyclable/reusable
Dr. Hauschka Cosmetic Bronze (Liquid)	Dr. Hauschka Cosmetics, Inc.	100% Natural Biodegradable Vegetable oil base
Dr. Hauschka Creams (Cream)	Dr. Hauschka Cosmetics, Inc.	100% Natural Biodegradable Vegetable oil base
Dr. Hauschka Eye Shadows (Cream)	Dr. Hauschka Cosmetics, Inc.	100% Natural Biodegradable
Dr. Hauschka Lip/Cheek Shades (Cream)	Dr. Hauschka Cosmetics, Inc.	100% Natural Biodegradable
Hygenia Natural Douche (Powder)	Women's Health Institute	100% Natural Biodegradable Dye-free
Ida Grae Cosmetic Brushes (Natural Bristle)	Nature's Colors, Ltd.	100% Natural bristles Biodegradable
Ida Grae Earth Eye/Lip Creme (Cream)	Nature's Colors, Ltd.	100% Natural Biodegradable Vegetable oil base
Ida Grae Earth Eyes Shades (Powder)	Nature's Colors, Ltd.	100% Natural Biodegradable Vegetable oil base
Ida Grae Earth Fragrances (Cream)	Nature's Colors, Ltd.	100% Natural Biodegradable Vegetable oil base
Ida Grae Earth Venus Moisturizer (Liquid)	Nature's Colors, Ltd.	100% Natural Biodegradable Vegetable oil base
Ida Grae Rouges (Powder)	Nature's Colors, Ltd.	100% Natural Biodegradable
Ida Grae Translucent Powder (Powder)	Nature's Colors, Ltd.	100% Natural Biodegradable

Product	Manufacturer	Description
Monoi Eau de Toilette (Liquid)	*Monoi, Inc.*	100% Natural Biodegradable Vegetable oil base
Natural Cosmetic Brushes (Natural Bristle)	*Aubrey Organics*	100% Natural bristles
Natural Cosmetic Sponge (Sponge)	*Aubrey Organics*	100% Natural Biodegradable
Natural Lips Lipsticks (Stick)	*Aubrey Organics*	100% Natural Biodegradable Vegetable oil base
O.B. Tampons (Rayon)	*McNeil-PPC*	Applicator-free Unscented
Orjene Elastin Foundation (Liquid)	*Orjene Natural Cosmetics*	Biodegradable Water base Unscented
Paul Penders Creme Make-Up (Cream)	*Paul Penders Products*	100% Natural Biodegradable
Paul Penders Eye Pencils (Stick)	*Paul Penders Products*	Biodegradable
Paul Penders Lipsticks (Stick)	*Paul Penders Products*	100% Natural Biodegradable
Paul Penders Mascara (Stick)	*Paul Penders Products*	Biodegradable
Silken Earth Blush Powders (Powder)	*Aubrey Organics*	100% Natural Biodegradable Vegetable oil base
Sombra Blushes (Cream)	*Sombra Cosmetics, Inc.*	Biodegradable Vegetable oil base
Sombra Foundation Make-Up (Cream)	*Sombra Cosmetics, Inc.*	Biodegradable Vegetable oil base
Tampax Tampons (Rayon/paper)	*Tampax*	Biodegradable applicator Unscented
Yeast-Guard (Powder)	*Women's Health Institute*	100% Natural Biodegradable Dye-free

The Bath-room

CHAPTER 5

The Broom Closet

T HE BROOM CLOSET is the repository of a wide variety of toxic and corrosive chemicals that will eventually make their way into the environment, either when you use them or when you throw away the last of what's left in the container.

- ◆ The word "nontoxic" on a product container means nothing under Federal law. There is no acceptable definition of the term.

- ◆ Septic tanks—used by 30 percent of American households—have been found to contain as many as 100 different toxic chemicals, virtually all of them from cleaning products. These leach into the ground.

Toilet bowl cleaners, fabric and upholstery cleaners, furniture polish, and spot removers can contain a variety of ingredients that, in a chemistry laboratory, would be handled with extreme caution. Around the home, however, they are generally handled as if harmless.

☞ Cleansers

Cleansers should be low in phosphates or contain no phosphates at all. Most general-purpose cleansers contain ammonia and perhaps ethanol. Although these are irritating to your skin and nose, they are not really a severe threat to the environment. Abrasive cleaners like scouring powder typically contain trisodium phosphate, which promotes the growth of algae in waterways.

Some bleaching cleaners contain chlorine. Others contain hydrogen peroxide or calcium hypochlorite, the same chem-

icals found in powdered bleaches. They too are irritating, but
are not considered a severe threat to the environment. Never
mix bleaching cleaners with regular cleaners, however; they
can produce toxic fumes. Read labels carefully.

Grease removers have organic solvents that are hazardous when they show up in your drinking water, as they
frequently do. Instead of a grease remover, try using a little more soap or detergent.

☞ Drain Openers

Most drain openers contain highly corrosive sodium and
potassium hydroxides, commonly known as lye. These
can react with organic chemicals in sewers and landfills,
creating more deadly products. Others contain concentrated acids, slightly better, but still a problem in the
sewer. Both types are hard on your metal pipes. The two
different types should never be mixed, because they can
produce toxic fumes. Again, read labels carefully.

☞ Disinfectants and Air Fresheners

Some disinfectants and mildew removers contain hydrogen peroxide, the same chemical found in powdered
bleach. They release free oxygen atoms, which kills
microorganisms. These can be very irritating to your skin,
but are not a serious pollution problem. Other disinfectants contain the much more toxic phenols. Air fresheners
typically do not remove odors, they simply mask them
with a heavier odor or numb your nasal passages so that
you don't smell anything.

☞ Furniture and Floor Polishes

Many furniture and floor polishes contain petrochemicals, a pollution problem, and nitrobenzene, which is
toxic. Polishes are also highly flammable. If you must use

commercial polishes, don't purchase them in aerosol cans. The propellants in such cans are hydrocarbons, a cause of air pollution and smog formation.

☞ Metal Polishes

Most metal polishes suffer from most of the same problems as furniture polishes. In addition, they usually contain phosphoric and sulfuric acids, skin irritants that contribute unnecessarily to indoor air pollution.

☞ Moth Balls

Moth balls contain para-dichlorobenzene, which causes cancer. They are also highly toxic. Avoid using them.

☞ Green Thinking

What You Can Do at Home
The most important thing is to avoid petrochemicals, formaldehyde, and similar products in cleaners of all sorts.

DO:

✔ Use alternatives that contain non-toxic ingredients (see "The Green Label Reader," page 225).

✔ Purchase cleaning agents in the largest containers possible and refill small spray bottles used for convenience.

DON'T:

✘ Don't mix various types of cleaners, such as toilet bowl cleaners and bleach. You'll produce toxic fumes.

☞ __Anatomy of a Green Product__

It is very important to be aware of the potent cleaning chemicals you can purchase at the supermarket, drug store and hardware store (See "The Green Label Reader," page 225). If you purchase according to the following general criteria, you will avoid many of the most common household and environmental hazards.

The most environmentally desirable products have the following characteristics:

All Cleaning Agents

100 percent natural (no synthetic chemicals), natural fibers (sponges), biodegradable, phosphate-free, chlorine-free; vegetable oil base, unscented, dye-free, concentrated.

Note: All products in this section are chlorine-free.

Product	Manufacturer	Description
General-Purpose Cleaners		
Allen's All-Purpose Cleaner (Liquid)	*Allen's Naturally*	Biodegradable Phosphate-free Unscented Dye-free Concentrated
Allen's Glass Cleaner (Liquid)	*Allen's Naturally*	Biodegradable Phosphate-free Unscented Dye-free
Allen's Spray Cleaner (Liquid)	*Allen's Naturally*	Biodegradable Phosphate-free Unscented Dye-free
Astonish Cream Cleaner (Liquid)	*A. Moss Chemical Corp.*	Biodegradable Phosphate-free
Bon Ami Cleaning Cake (Bar)	*Bon Ami/Faultless Starch Co.*	Biodegradable Phosphate-free
Cellulose Sponges (Cellulose)	*O-Cel-O Sponges*	Natural fiber Biodegradable Reusable
Cloverdale Cleaner (Liquid)	*Cloverdale*	Biodegradable Phosphate-free Concentrated
De-Solv-It (Liquid)	*Orange-Sol, Inc.*	Biodegradable Low-phosphate Recyclable packaging
Earth Guard All Purpose Cleaner (Liquid)	*Omega Products*	Biodegradable Concentrated
Ecover Cream Cleaner (Liquid)	*Mercantile Food Co.*	100% Natural Biodegradable Phosphate-free Vegetable oil base
Ecover Floor Soap (Liquid)	*Mercantile Food Co.*	100% Natural Biodegradable Phosphate-free Vegetable oil base

The Broom Closet

Product	Manufacturer	Description
Ecover Heavy Duty Hand Cleaner (Liquid)	*Mercantile Food Co.*	100% Natural Biodegradable Phosphate-free Vegetable oil base
Ecover Toilet Cleaner (Liquid)	*Mercantile Food Co.*	100% Natural Biodegradable Phosphate-free Vegetable oil base
Gunk Swab Concrete Cleaner (Liquid)	*Radiator Specialty*	Biodegradable Phosphate-free
Homesteaders Hand Soap (Cream)	*Homesteader & Arnold Co.*	100% Natural Biodegradable Phosphate-free Vegetable oil base Dye-free
K-Mart Oil Soap (Liquid)	*Zoe Chemical Co.*	Phosphate-free Vegetable oil base
Kleen All-Purpose Cleaner (Liquid)	*Mountain Fresh Products*	Biodegradable Phosphate-free Dye-free Concentrated
Lightening Sweet 'n Clean (Liquid)	*Lightening Products*	100% Natural Biodegradable Vegetable oil base
Murphy Oil Soap (Liquid)	*Murphy Phoenix Co.*	Phosphate-free Vegetable oil base

Deodorizers and Disinfectants

Product	Manufacturer	Description
Cedar Fresh Eco-Safe Closet Freshener (Wood)	*Arbor American Corp.*	100% Natural Biodegradable Reusable
Cedar Fresh Stick-Ups Air Freshener (Wood)	*Arbor American Corp.*	100% Natural Biodegradable Reusable
Moth-Away Herbal Sachets (Powder)	*Richards Homewares*	100% Natural Biodegradable Reusable

CHAPTER 6

The Workshop

MANY TOXIC WASTE problems arise in the workshop where a wide variety of toxic chemicals are used routinely and, perhaps more important, routinely disposed of improperly.

- We use 3 million gallons of paint every day. On a yearly basis, that's 1 billion gallons—enough to fill a lake 2 miles long, 2 miles wide, and 20 feet deep.

- According to a San Francisco survey, paints and paint products—including thinners, solvents, stains, and finishes—account for 60 percent of the hazardous wastes dumped by individuals.

- Americans throw away 2.5 billion pounds of batteries every year, contaminating landfills with a variety of toxic metals.

In addition to being toxic, most of the chemicals used in the basement and workshop are highly flammable. Improper storage of such chemicals, especially close to water heaters, is a major cause of fires.

☞ Paints and Solvents

Oil-Based Paints

Oil-based paints, thinners, solvents, and varnishes contain a variety of hydrocarbons, including benzene (a carcinogen), which can cause serious health problems with prolonged exposure (see "The Green Label Reader," page

225). These hydrocarbons also escape into the air when the paint dries after use or when they leak out of an improperly sealed container. They can be a major contributor to air pollution, reacting with other pollutants in the air to form ozone and photochemical smog. California has banned the sale of oil-based paint products beginning in the mid-1990s. Other regions with severe smog problems are likely to follow suit—but you can begin by avoiding them now.

Paint strippers contain a variety of hydrocarbons that will dissolve dried paints, and also represent a serious hazard. They are more difficult to avoid, but their use can be minimized by sanding, scraping, using electric heat guns when feasible. *Do not use these techniques to strip paint containing lead; they will create lead fumes or fine particles of lead that can be inhaled.*

Anti-rust paints contain many of the same hydrocarbon ingredients. Water-based anti-rust paints are available in many stores and from mail-order catalogs (see chapter 14).

Disposal

Do not throw oil-based paints and thinners in the trash, dump them into sewers, or pour them down the drain. The best solution is to use them up. Alternatively, if there is enough left, give them to a friend or painter, or perhaps donate them to a charity that needs them. If you must dispose of them, take them to a hazardous waste disposal center. (Contact your local sanitation department for more information.)

Latex Paints

Latex or water-based paints are a desirable alternative because they do not contain the hydrocarbons found in oil-based paints. But take care in using them, especially those with added ingredients, such as fungicides. Some fungicidal paints, for example, contain mercury, an environmental and health hazard. Alternative water-based paints containing beeswax, carnauba wax, and plant extracts and gums are becoming increasingly available, as are fungicide-free latex paints.

Disposal

Latex-based paints are easy to dispose of. Allow the residue in the can to sit outside with the lid off until they have turned solid. They can then be disposed of in the trash without danger of their contents leaching into water supplies. Never pour them down the drain.

☞ Spray Paints

Avoid purchasing spray cans of paint whenever possible. Their propellants contribute to air pollution. Also, inhaling the fine particles of the spray can cause respiratory problems. If you must do spray painting, consider the purchase of a compressed air sprayer, and wear a mask.

☞ Adhesives

Adhesives, sealants, caulks, and glues are other sources of hydrocarbon emissions. White glues often will serve as a suitable alternative. If you have to use adhesives, however, keep them tightly sealed while they are stored and use them all up.

Disposal

Do not dispose of leftover petroleum-based glues and adhesives in the trash unless they have dried out completely and are solid. If still in liquid form, take them to a toxic waste disposal center. Once solidified, water-based glues can probably be safely thrown in the regular trash since they do not redisolve when exposed to precipitation.

☞ Building Materials

Pressure-treated wood is impregnated with materials like pentachlorophenol, creosote, and arsenic compounds that kill or repel termites and other insects, as well as bacteria that can degrade the wood. These chemicals are very toxic to humans and animals as well as to insects. There are at least 40 hazardous waste sites where pentachlorophenol and its contaminants are stored are on an EPA list of extremely hazardous sites marked for priority cleanup.

Where insect or bacterial resistance is important—when wood is exposed to soil or water, for example—pressure treatment is effective, but great care should be taken when handling pressure-treated stock. Use gloves during construction; wear clothing that will prevent the chemicals from reaching the skin; wash those clothes separately from other clothing. Do not breathe the sawdust produced when cutting it—use a mask. Wash yourself thoroughly after using the wood. Painting the wood will help seal in the chemicals and reduce the threat.

Many types of plywood, chipboard, particle board, and paneling are made with adhesives that contain formaldehyde, a health and environmental hazard. When new, such materials should not be exposed to high temperatures, which accelerate the release of formaldehyde.

☞ Batteries

With the growing use of portable radios and other personal electronic gear, disposable batteries are becoming an increasingly important source of pollution. They contain a variety of toxic metals—including cadmium, lead, lithium, manganese dioxide, mercury, silver, and zinc—that can cause neurological and other health problems. When batteries corrode in landfills, these metals leach out and pollute groundwater. This has already become a problem in Japan where large numbers of batteries are used and landfills generally are not lined to prevent liquids from escaping.

The manufacture of disposable batteries also pollutes and is energy-intensive: producing them consumes about 50 times as much energy as the batteries produce. Finally, the button-sized batteries used in watches, calculators, and other items are a hazard to young children, who might swallow them. A battery can burn a hole in a child's intestines.

Use Rechargeable Batteries

The best alternative to disposable batteries is rechargeable ones. Although their initial purchase price is significantly higher than that of disposables, they ultimately prove substantially cheaper because they can be reused—usually more than 100 times.

Disposal

The metals in batteries can readily be recycled, but only a handful of pilot programs now exist. Never place batteries in trash that will be incinerated; burning them will disperse the toxic metals through the air. The best solution is to store used batteries in a safe location in the basement, then bring them to a toxic waste disposal drive or center.

☞ Green Thinking

What You Can Do at Home

Oil-based shop products should be avoided whenever possible. And toxic chemicals should never be discarded in the trash.

DO:
- ✔ Use water-based paints, stains, and varnishes.
- ✔ Keep all cans and bottles in the workshop sealed tight to prevent escape of toxic materials.
- ✔ Take leftover paints, glues, sealants, and so forth to a proper disposal facility for disposal. Don't throw them in the trash or down the drain.
- ✔ Purchase rechargeable batteries.

DON'T:
- ✘ Don't wash paintbrushes and other tools outside, where the paints can escape into groundwater.
- ✘ Don't throw used batteries in the trash or incinerate them.

☞ Anatomy of a Green Product

Reading labels is particularly important in the workshop to avoid toxic chemicals. Check "The Green Label Reader," Page 225, if you aren't sure about the environmental or health effects of particular components in the products you intend to buy.

The most environmentally desirable products have the following characteristics:

Paint Products
100 percent natural (no synthetic chemicals), formaldehyde-free, no petrochemicals, no hydrocarbons, water base. Wood preservatives: no creosote, arsenicals. Strippers: no methyl chloride.

Adhesives
100 percent natural (no synthetic chemicals), formaldehyde-free, no petrochemicals, no hydrocarbons, water base.

Note: This section contains a minimal number of product listings; most readily available workshop and building products contain dangerous chemicals. Many commercial paint products, for example, contain formaldehyde, fungicides, mercury, and other substances harmful to people and the environment. Adhesives frequently contain formaldehyde, phenols, and naphthalene, all of which are problematic (see "The Green Label Reader," page 225). Chapter 14 provides a broad assortment of mail-order products for the workshop that meet stringent environmental criteria.

Product	Manufacturer	Description

Paint Products

Product	Manufacturer	Description
High Build Sealer (Liquid)	*BonaKemi U.S.A.*	Formaldehyde-free Water base
Pacific One Waterborne Finish (Liquid)	*BonaKemi U.S.A.*	Formaldehyde-free Water base
Pacific Strong D-503 Finish (Liquid)	*BonaKemi U.S.A.*	Formaldehyde-free Water base

Adhesives

Product	Manufacturer	Description
Crayola Art & Craft Glue (Liquid)	*Binney & Smith*	Water base
DuraFix (Liquid)	*Ross Adhesives*	Formaldehyde-free Water base
Elmer's Carpenter Glue (Liquid)	*Borden, Inc.*	Water base
Elmer's Glue All (Liquid)	*Borden, Inc.*	Water base
Ross Kid's Glue (Liquid)	*Ross Adhesives*	Formaldehyde-free Water base
Sobo (Liquid)	*Slomons Group*	Water base

The Work-Shop

CHAPTER 7

The Yard and Pet Supplies

P ESTICIDES, HERBICIDES, AND FERTILIZERS are the biggest environmental problems in the garden. Pesticides are the most toxic materials used by homeowners, and they represent a severe threat to the environment.

- ◆ The average American homeowner uses 5 to 10 pounds of pesticides on his lawn every year, a total of about 50 million pounds. Homeowners use 10 times more pesticide per acre than farmers.

- ◆ We spend a billion dollars per year on 83 brands of pesticides containing as many as 400 separate ingredients.

- ◆ Roughly 80 percent of the pesticides sold in supermarkets and hardware stores have not been tested for causing cancer, and most have also not been studied for producing birth defects, genetic damage, and other health effects.

- ◆ According to the EPA, in 1988 sales of pesticides for home use totaled $560 million, herbicides $350 million, and fungicides $110 million.

☞ Pesticides

Environmental Effects

Pesticides, herbicides, and fertilizers used on lawns and in gardens are often washed away into sewers, where they join with oil from city streets, lead emitted by cars, animal feces, and a host of other materials. This "non-point-source" pollution then usually travels directly into waterways without passing through any sewage treatment facilities. Once there, it can poison fish and other wildlife, as well as kill microorganisms that the fish eat. Non-point-source pollution is now one of the most important causes of water pollution in America. It accounts for 76 percent of pollution in severely polluted lakes, 65 percent in severely polluted rivers, and 45 percent in severely polluted estuaries. It is estimated that as much as 21 million pounds of pesticides—more than 40 percent of the amount used by homeowners—reaches groundwater or surface water before degrading.

Many experts also think that lawn pesticides kill songbirds when they ingest earthworms tainted by the chemicals. Freshly sprayed lawns are also a hazard to children and pets, when they come in contact with the chemicals. Of course, storage of pesticides in the home poses a risk for young children, who may inadvertently drink them or spill them on themselves. And finally, throwing that bit of leftover pesticide into the trash contaminates landfills, posing an additional threat to groundwater. Especially of concern are the extremely toxic organo-phosphates and the arsenicals and chlorinated hydrocarbons, which persist in the environment for long periods of time.

Use the Minimum Amount

The average homeowner generally assumes that if a little pesticide is good, a lot is even better. That is certainly not the case. If a given amount of a pesticide will kill off 99 percent of the insects in an area, then doubling or tripling the amount used is not going to make much difference. The green consumer will always use the minimum amount necessary to do the job. Better yet, a variety of much safer alternatives are available to replace synthetic pesticides in part or altogether.

Consider Alternatives

Some problems in the garden can be eliminated manually. Pests like caterpillars, snails, and sawfly larvae can often simply be picked off by hand and disposed of, and aphids can be wiped off plants with your hands (wear gloves) or a stream of water. Diseased leaves on plants can also be picked and burned or thrown in the trash; don't put them in your compost pile or you may simply spread the disease. You should also make an effort to encourage natural pest controls. One way to accomplish this is to provide nesting sites and habitats for frogs, birds, and insects like the praying mantis, ladybugs, syrphid flies, and soldier beetles, which all prey on pests.

Several alternatives to synthetic pesticides are also available. Stale beer, for example, can be set out in a bowl at night to attract and drown slugs. Some insecticidal soaps are a good way to kill crickets, mealybugs, aphids, rose slugs, earwigs, spittlebugs, whiteflies, scales, and other insects. Certain natural oil sprays will kill mites, mealybugs, scale insects, and whitefly larvae on trees, shrubs, evergreens, and other ornamental plants.

Other alternatives can also be used inside the house. Ants, for example, can occasionally be controlled by sprinkling barriers of boric acid, bone meal, or talcum powder across their trails. Cockroaches, persistent though they are, can sometimes be controlled by sprinkling borax around the refrigerator, stove, dishwasher, and ducts. Boric acid can also be combined with sugar and flour to make a powder that cockroaches will take back to their nests, where it will poison others. Moths can be controlled by storing woolens in cedar chests or closets or in tightly sealed plastic bags.

Disposal

Never place leftover pesticides in the trash or pour them down the drain. Either action runs the risk of polluting surface and groundwater. Call your local sanitation department for information on how to dispose of them.

☞ Herbicides

Herbicides contain chlorinated organic compounds that are very irritating to the skin. Some also contain highly toxic dioxins. Many of the chlorinated compounds persist in the environment for long periods and accumulate in the fatty tissues of animals, causing a health risk for the animals and for humans who eat them.

What's the alternative? Choose one of the herbicides in the following listings. Or, do it the old-fashioned way—pluck weeds by hand. On the lawn, fertilizing early in the spring will speed the growth of grass, allowing it to become tall enough to choke out many weeds. Don't cut the grass very short, either; keeping it long will help control weeds.

Disposal

Never pour herbicides down the drain or dispose of them in trash. Take them to a toxic waste disposal center or call your local sanitation department for instructions.

☞ Fertilizers

Plants grow by extracting nutrients from the soil and incorporating them into their stalks and leaves. A certain amount of fertilization may be necessary in some climates, but most homeowners fertilize too often and too heavily, so that excess runs off with rainfall and pollutes groundwater and rivers. In surface waters, fertilizers promote the unrestrained growth of algae and other microorganisms; when they die, their decomposition uses up the oxygen in the water, suffocating fish and other wildlife.

If you live in the north, you should only need to fertilize twice a year, preferably in the fall and spring when plants can make maximum use of the nutrients. If you live in the south, with its longer growing season, a third application may be necessary.

Make Your Own

Ideally, your grass clipping, weeds, leaves, vegetable scraps, and other organic material should go into a compost pile (do not include diseased branches and leaves). A compost pile accelerates the natural degradation of leaves and other plant material that occurs in forests. It also will help to reduce the solid waste burden—some studies have shown that leaf material and food wastes comprise 33 percent of household trash.

The minimum size for biological activity in a compost pile is about three feet square. It can be larger, but should not be much higher than five feet—the weight will compress the interior too much for effective bacterial activity. The compost should be kept damp but not soggy, and should be turned over with a shovel or pitchfork every three or four days to minimize odors and speed up the decay. One big advantage of compost is that, when applied to the lawn or garden, it decomposes slowly, releasing nutrients at a rate that is nearly ideal for plants to absorb them.

Disposal

Disposal of fertilizers should never be an issue: simply use it all up on your lawn. If you have some that you have no use for, give it to a friend or neighbor.

☞ Watering _____

In order to cut down on water usage, consider watering your lawn or garden first thing in the morning. Midday watering wastes a large amount of water through evaporation and watering in the evening can cause mildew. Avoid watering lawns that have turned brown because of drought conditions; the lawn won't come back until the drought is over, and you'll just be wasting water.

Grow grasses and plants that are native to your area—they won't require excessive watering. Finally, try growing plants that do well in drought conditions.

☞ Cleaning Up_____

Most people use plastic trash bags for leaves, lawn clippings, and other debris from the yard. The bags do not degrade in landfills—even when they are labeled biodegradable—and they slow the decomposition of the yard wastes (see "A Guide to Environmental Issues"—Plastics entry). Large paper bags are an excellent alternative.

☞ Pet Supplies

We all love our pets. Americans own and adore turtles, horses, snakes, pigs, monkeys, and a host of less common species. But above all else, we love our cats and dogs: we own 115 million of them. Although we love our pets, we often don't take care of them as well as we should. In our efforts to socialize them for indoor life, we often subject them to chemicals that are not good for their health or for our own.

Fleas and Ticks

Fleas and ticks are the most common infestations of dogs and cats, and they can be both a nuisance and a health threat. The fleas irritate animals and they also carry bacteria and viruses that produce several illnesses, including skin infections, tapeworms, anemia, and allergies.

Our first thought when our animals get fleas is to put on a flea and tick collar. Every year, we buy more than 50 million of them, then end up dumping them into landfills. These plastic bands contain very toxic chemicals that escape from the collar over a period of time, killing the pests. The most common of the chemicals include piperonyl butoxide, which can cause liver damage; dichlorvos or DDVP, which can cause cancer, nerve damage, and birth defects; and carbaryl, which may cause birth defects. These chemicals are bad for animals or humans who come in contact with them. When the collars are discarded, the pesticides continue to escape, and can contaminate groundwater sources.

Another pesticide frequently used by veterinarians to get rid of fleas is fenthion. In 1988, workers at a Georgia veterinary office developed nerve damage from persistent exposure to fenthion, so continued exposure of your dog is not advised.

What Are the Alternatives?

Some herbal flea repellents (see product listings) are available, and you might try one. But if fleas attack, the first course of action is to bathe the animal. You will almost certainly have to disinfect the house thoroughly in order to remove both fleas and eggs. Wash the animal's bedding in hot water and vacuum carpets thoroughly.

If you must use chemicals to sterilize your house in order to prevent reinfestation, use a pump-type spray to apply the pesticide where it is needed rather than an aerosol "bomb" that coats all surfaces in the house. Follow directions and be careful not to mix pesticides.

Cat Litter

If you have an indoor cat or kittens that are still being trained to go outside, cat litter is essential. These mineral-based adsorbents are relatively innocuous in themselves, and are not generally considered an environmental threat. Added scents are unnecessary, and may hide the fact that your litter box needs to be emptied or changed.

Litter Dust

Some studies have shown that litter dust contributes to ongoing respiratory infections in cats. They also recommend using litter that is as dust-free as possible.

Pet Food

A variety of pet foods are available for both cats and dogs. While a discussion of animal nutrition is beyond the scope of this book, from an environmental standpoint, choose packaging that can be recycled or reused. That generally means cans, cardboard, and large paper sacks. Avoid individual servings packed in foil/paper wrappers. Not only is extra packaging required, but the packaging itself is undesirable since it is not recyclable and does not degrade in landfills.

☞ Green Thinking _____

What You Can Do at Home

Yard

In general terms, it is best to use natural products on your lawn and garden rather than synthetics. And toxic chemicals should never be discarded in trash.

DO:

✔ Dispose of your lawn and garden clippings, as well as household vegetable scraps, in a compost pile.

✔ Use natural alternatives to pesticides for controlling lawn and garden pests—use the pests' own natural enemies to help control them.

✔ Provide nesting sites for birds and insects that will control pests. Food and water for these predators are also important.

✔ If it is absolutely necessary to water, use soaker hoses and drip irrigation instead of sprinklers whenever possible. These waste much less water.

✔ Water early in the day to avoid excessive evaporation.

DON'T:

✘ If you must use synthetic pesticides, herbicides, and fertilizers, don't use more than the minimum amounts.

✘ Don't overwater your lawn; aside from wasting water, you may kill the roots.

☞ Green Thinking

What You Can Do at Home

Pet Supplies

Try to avoid increasing the chemical burden in and around your home in your efforts to keep your pets pest-free. Use the most benign approaches first, and only later experiment with more potent approaches.

DO:

✔ Use natural alternatives to pet collars and pesticides.

✔ As with all food products, avoid foil/paper pet food pouches—the packaging materials cannot be recycled.

DON'T:

✘ Don't use "bombs" when you must use a pesticide to kill fleas and ticks. Instead, use pump sprays in limited areas.

✘ Don't buy litter on the basis of its odor-masking abilities—dust-free should be your major criteria.

☞ Anatomy of a Green Product

Reading labels is particularly important when it comes to garden supplies, given the chemical feast you might bring home. Be especially on the lookout for synthetic and petroleum-based ingredients. For pet supplies, also beware of potentially harmful components.

The most environmentally desirable products have the following characteristics:

Yard

Pest Control Products and Fertilizers
100 percent natural (no synthetic chemicals), biodegradable, no organo-phosphates, no arsenicals, no chlorinated hydrocarbons, concentrated.

Lawn Bags
Paper only.

Pet Supplies

Flea and Tick Products
100 percent natural (no synthetic chemicals), biodegradable, no organo-phosphates, no arsenicals, no chlorinated hydrocarbons, reusable packaging.

Regular Pet Shampoos
100 percent natural (no synthetic chemicals), biodegradable, vegetable oil base.

Cat Litter
Dust-free, no perfumes.

Product	Manufacturer	Description

Pest-Control Products

Product	Manufacturer	Description
African Violet Insect Killer (Liquid)	*Safer*	100% Natural Biodegradable No organo-phosphates No arsenicals No chlorinated hydrocarbons
Aphid, Whitefly Killer (Liquid)	*Safer*	100% Natural Biodegradable No organo-phosphates No arsenicals No chlorinated hydrocarbons
Aphid-Mite Attack (Liquid)	*Ringer*	100% Natural Biodegradable No organo-phosphates No arsenicals No chlorinated hydrocarbons
B.t. Caterpillar Killer (Liquid)	*Safer*	100% Natural Biodegradable No organo-phosphates No arsenicals No chlorinated hydrocarbons Concentrated
Clandosan Nematode Control (Granular)	*Safer*	100% Natural Biodegradable No organo-phosphates No arsenicals No chlorinated hydrocarbons
Colorado Potato Beetle Beater (Liquid)	*Bonide*	Biodegradable No organo-phosphates No arsenicals No chlorinated hydrocarbons
Crawling Insect Attack (Liquid)	*Ringer*	100% Natural Biodegradable No organo-phosphates No arsenicals No chlorinated hydrocarbons
Dipel Dust (Powder)	*Bonide*	Biodegradable No organo-phosphates No arsenicals No chlorinated hydrocarbons

Yard and Pet

Product	Manufacturer	Description
Dis-Patch (Powder/Granular)	*Ringer*	100% Natural Biodegradable No organo-phosphates No arsenicals No chlorinated hydrocarbons
ENTIRE Flea & Tick Spray (Liquid)	*Safer*	100% Natural Biodegradable No organo-phosphates No arsenicals No chlorinated hydrocarbons
ENTIRE Insect Killer for Trees (Liquid)	*Safer*	100% Natural Biodegradable No organo-phosphates No arsenicals No chlorinated hydrocarbons
ENTIRE Insect Killer for Yards (Liquid)	*Safer*	100% Natural Biodegradable No organo-phosphates No arsenicals No chlorinated hydrocarbons
Early Alert Trapstix (Paper)	*Safer*	100% Natural Biodegradable No organo-phosphates No arsenicals No chlorinated hydrocarbons
Flea & Tick Attack (Liquid)	*Ringer*	100% Natural Biodegradable No organo-phosphates No arsenicals No chlorinated hydrocarbons
Flying Insect Attack (Bars)	*Ringer*	100% Natural Biodegradable No organo-phosphates No arsenicals No chlorinated hydrocarbons
Garden Dust (Powder)	*Bonide*	Biodegradable No organo-phosphates No arsenicals No chlorinated hydrocarbons

Product	Manufacturer	Description
Garden Fungicide (Liquid)	*Safer*	100% Natural Biodegradable No organo-phosphates No arsenicals No chlorinated hydrocarbons
Garden Insect Killer (Liquid)	*Safer*	100% Natural Biodegradable No organo-phosphates No arsenicals No chlorinated hydrocarbons
Garden Insecticidal Soap (Liquid)	*Safer*	100% Natural Biodegradable No organo-phosphates No arsenicals No chlorinated hydrocarbons Concentrated
Grasshopper Control (Granular)	*Safer*	100% Natural Biodegradable No organo-phosphates No arsenicals No chlorinated hydrocarbons
Green Ban for Plants (Powder)	*Mulgum Hollow Farm*	100% Natural Biodegradable No organo-phosphates No arsenicals No chlorinated hydrocarbons
Grub Attack (Powder/Granular)	*Ringer*	100% Natural Biodegradable No organo-phosphates No arsenicals No chlorinated hydrocarbons
Grub Killer (Powder)	*Safer*	100% Natural Biodegradable No organo-phosphates No arsenicals No chlorinated hydrocarbons
Insect Soap for Fruits & Vegetables (Liquid)	*Safer*	100% Natural Biodegradable No organo-phosphates No arsenicals No chlorinated hydrocarbons

Yard and Pet

Product	Manufacturer	Description
Insect Soap for Houseplants (Liquid)	*Safer*	100% Natural Biodegradable No organo-phosphates No arsenicals No chlorinated hydrocarbons Concentrated
Insect Soap for Roses & Flowers (Liquid)	*Safer*	100% Natural Biodegradable No organo-phosphates No arsenicals No chlorinated hydrocarbons
Japanese Beetle Killer (Liquid)	*Safer*	100% Natural Biodegradable No organo-phosphates No arsenicals No chlorinated hydrocarbons
Mite Killer (Liquid)	*Safer*	100% Natural Biodegradable No organo-phosphates No arsenicals No chlorinated hydrocarbons
Moss & Algae Killer for Decks (Liquid)	*Safer*	100% Natural Biodegradable No organo-phosphates No arsenicals No chlorinated hydrocarbons
Moss Killer for Lawns (Liquid)	*Safer*	100% Natural Biodegradable No organo-phosphates No arsenicals No chlorinated hydrocarbons Concentrated
Pyrenone Crop Spray (Liquid)	*Bonide*	Biodegradable No organo-phosphates No arsenicals No chlorinated hydrocarbons
Rotenone (Powder/Liquid)	*Bonide*	Biodegradable No organo-phosphates No arsenicals No chlorinated hydrocarbons

Product	Manufacturer	Description
Rotenone/Pyrethrin Spray (Liquid)	*Bonide*	Biodegradable No organo-phosphates No arsenicals No chlorinated hydrocarbons
Safer Traps-Housefly (Plastic)	*Safer*	100% Natural Biodegradable No organo-phosphates No arsenicals No chlorinated hydrocarbons
Safer Traps-Japanese Beetles (Paper)	*Safer*	100% Natural Biodegradable No organo-phosphates No arsenicals No chlorinated hydrocarbons
SharpShooter Weed Killer (Liquid)	*Safer*	100% Natural Biodegradable No organo-phosphates No arsenicals No chlorinated hydrocarbons
Vegetable Insect Attack (Powder)	*Ringer*	100% Natural Biodegradable No organo-phosphates No arsenicals No chlorinated hydrocarbons
Wasp & Hornet Attack (Liquid)	*Ringer*	100% Natural Biodegradable No organo-phosphates No arsenicals No chlorinated hydrocarbons
Yard & Garden Insect Attack (Liquid)	*Ringer*	100% Natural Biodegradable No organo-phosphates No arsenicals No chlorinated hydrocarbons
Zap Ant & Roach Powder (Powder)	*EcoSafe Laboratories*	100% Natural Biodegradable No organo-phosphates No arsenicals No chlorinated hydrocarbons

Yard
and
Pet

Product	Manufacturer	Description

Fertilizers

Product	Manufacturer	Description
Berry Booster (Powder)	*Ringer*	100% Natural Biodegradable No organo-phosphates No arsenicals No chlorinated hydrocarbons
Brown Leaf Compost Maker (Powder)	*Ringer*	100% Natural Biodegradable No organo-phosphates No arsenicals No chlorinated hydrocarbons
Compost Plus (Powder)	*Ringer*	100% Natural Biodegradable No organo-phosphates No arsenicals No chlorinated hydrocarbons
Flower Garden Restore (Powder)	*Ringer*	100% Natural Biodegradable No organo-phosphates No arsenicals No chlorinated hydrocarbons
ForEverGreen Plant Protectant (Liquid)	*Safer*	100% Natural Biodegradable No organo-phosphates No arsenicals No chlorinated hydrocarbons
Fruit Tree Booster (Powder)	*Ringer*	100% Natural Biodegradable No organo-phosphates No arsenicals No chlorinated hydrocarbons
Grass Clippings Compost Maker (Powder)	*Ringer*	100% Natural Biodegradable No organo-phosphates No arsenicals No chlorinated hydrocarbons
Grass-Patch Growing System (Powder)	*Ringer*	100% Natural Biodegradable No organo-phosphates No arsenicals No chlorinated hydrocarbons

Product	Manufacturer	Description
Lawn Restore (Powder)	*Ringer*	100% Natural Biodegradable No organo-phosphates No arsenicals No chlorinated hydrocarbons
Leafclean & Lustre (Liquid)	*Safer*	100% Natural Biodegradable No organo-phosphates No arsenicals No chlorinated hydrocarbons
Naturelease for Tomatoes (Powder)	*Ringer*	100% Natural Biodegradable No organo-phosphates No arsenicals No chlorinated hydrocarbons
Potato Booster (Powder)	*Ringer*	100% Natural Biodegradable No organo-phosphates No arsenicals No chlorinated hydrocarbons
ReStart Starter Fertilizer (Powder)	*Ringer*	100% Natural Biodegradable No organo-phosphates No arsenicals No chlorinated hydrocarbons
Ready-Made Compost (Powder)	*Ringer*	100% Natural Biodegradable No organo-phosphates No arsenicals No chlorinated hydrocarbons
Restore for Bulbs (Powder)	*Ringer*	100% Natural Biodegradable No organo-phosphates No arsenicals No chlorinated hydrocarbons
Restore for Foliage Plants (Powder)	*Ringer*	100% Natural Biodegradable No organo-phosphates No arsenicals No chlorinated hydrocarbons

Yard and Pet

Product	Manufacturer	Description
Rose Restore (Powder)	*Ringer*	100% Natural Biodegradable No organo-phosphates No arsenicals No chlorinated hydrocarbons
Shrub Restore (Powder)	*Ringer*	100% Natural Biodegradable No organo-phosphates No arsenicals No chlorinated hydrocarbons
Strawberry Booster (Powder)	*Ringer*	100% Natural Biodegradable No organo-phosphates No arsenicals No chlorinated hydrocarbons
Stump Remover (Powder)	*Ringer*	100% Natural Biodegradable No organo-phosphates No arsenicals No chlorinated hydrocarbons
Tomato Restore (Powder)	*Ringer*	100% Natural Biodegradable No organo-phosphates No arsenicals No chlorinated hydrocarbons
Vegetable Garden Restore (Powder)	*Ringer*	100% Natural Biodegradable No organo-phosphates No arsenicals No chlorinated hydrocarbons
Winter Garden Soil Restore (Powder)	*Ringer*	100% Natural Biodegradable No organo-phosphates No arsenicals No chlorinated hydrocarbons
WinterStore for Lawns (Powder)	*Ringer*	100% Natural Biodegradable No organo-phosphates No arsenicals No chlorinated hydrocarbons

Product	Manufacturer	Description

Pet-Care and Products

Product	Manufacturer	Description
Attack Conditioning Pet Shampo (Liquid)	*Ringer*	100% Natural Biodegradable No organo-phosphates No arsenicals No chlorinated hydrocarbons
Cat-Ex Flea Treatment (Liquid)	*Pet Organics*	Biodegradable No organo-phosphates No arsenicals No chlorinated hydrocarbons
Coat Conditioner for Dogs (Liquid)	*Safer*	100% Natural Biodegradable No organo-phosphates No arsenicals No chlorinated hydrocarbons
Dog-Ex Flea Treatment (Liquid)	*Pet Organics*	Biodegradable No organo-phosphates No arsenicals No chlorinated hydrocarbons
ENTIRE Flea & Tick Spray (Liquid)	*Safer*	100% Natural Biodegradable No organo-phosphates No arsenicals No chlorinated hydrocarbons
Flea & Tick Attack (Liquid)	*Ringer*	100% Natural Biodegradable No organo-phosphates No arsenicals No chlorinated hydrocarbons
Flea-Relief (Liquid)	*Dr. Goodpet Products*	100% Natural Biodegradable No organo-phosphates No arsenicals No chlorinated hydrocarbons
Gentle Dragon Wormer-Cats & Dogs (Powder)	*EcoSafe Laboratories*	100% Natural Biodegradable No organo-phosphates No arsenicals No chlorinated hydrocarbons

Yard
and
Pet

Product	Manufacturer	Description
Golden Lemon Shampoo-Dog/Cat (Liquid)	Safer	100% Natural Biodegradable No organo-phosphates No arsenicals No chlorinated hydrocarbons
Green Ban Dog Shampoo (Liquid)	Mulgum Hollow Farm	100% Natural Biodegradable No organo-phosphates No arsenicals No chlorinated hydrocarbons
Green Ban Flea Powder (Powder)	Mulgum Hollow Farm	100% Natural Biodegradable No organo-phosphates No arsenicals No chlorinated hydrocarbons
Herbal Animal Shampoo Concentrate (Liquid)	EcoSafe Laboratories	100% Natural Biodegradable No organo-phosphates No arsenicals No chlorinated hydrocarbons Concentrated
Indoor Flea Guard (Liquid)	Safer	100% Natural Biodegradable No organo-phosphates No arsenicals No chlorinated hydrocarbons
Kleen Pet Flea Shampoo (Liquid)	Pet Organics	Biodegradable No organo-phosphates No arsenicals No chlorinated hydrocarbons
Lightening Cat Shampoo (Liquid)	Lightening Products	100% Natural Biodegradable Vegetable oil Base
Lightening Cat Spray (Liquid)	Lightening Products	100% Natural Biodegradable Vegetable oil base
Lightening Dog Shampoo (Liquid)	Lightening Products	100% Natural Biodegradable Vegetable oil base

Product	Manufacturer	Description
Lightening Sweet & Clean (Liquid)	*Lightening Products*	100% Natural Biodegradable No organo-phosphates No arsenicals No chlorinated hydrocarbons Vegetable oil base
Nature's Gate Pet Shampoo (Liquid)	*Nature's Gate/Levlad, Inc.*	100% Natural Biodegradable Vegetable oil base
Organimals Dip & Creme Rinse (Liquid)	*Aubrey Organics*	100% Natural Biodegradable Vegetable oil base
Organimals Grooming Spray (Liquid)	*Aubrey Organics*	100% Natural Biodegradable Vegetable oil base
Organimals Pet Shampoo (Liquid)	*Aubrey Organics*	100% Natural Biodegradable Vegetable oil base
POW Herbal Flea Powder (Powder)	*EcoSafe Laboratories*	100% Natural Biodegradable No organo-phosphates No arsenicals No chlorinated hydrocarbons
Pet Guard Herbal Flea Collar (Liquid/Fabric)	*Pet Guard*	100% Natural Biodegradable No organo-phosphates No arsenicals No chlorinated hydrocarbons Rechargeable/reusable
Rechargeable Herbal Flea Collar (Liquid/Fabric)	*EcoSafe Laboratories*	100% Natural Biodegradable No organo-phosphates No arsenicals No chlorinated hydrocarbons Reusable
Safer Pet Odor Eliminator (Liquid)	*Safer*	100% Natural Biodegradable No organo-phosphates No arsenicals No chlorinated hydrocarbons

Yard and Pet

Product	Manufacturer	Description
Safer's Flea Soap for Dogs/Cats (Liquid)	*Safer*	100% Natural Biodegradable No organo-phosphates No arsenicals No chlorinated hydrocarbons
Skin & Coat Conditioner (Liquid)	*Pet Organics*	Biodegradable No organo-phosphates No arsenicals No chlorinated hydrocarbons
Spritz Dog/Cat Coat Enhancer (Liquid)	*EcoSafe Laboratories*	100% Natural Biodegradable

Cat Litter

Product	Manufacturer	Description
CatWorks Premium Cat Litter (Powder)	*Purina Mills, Inc.*	100% Natural Biodegradable 99% Dust-free
Good Mews Cat Litter w/ Cedar (Powder)	*Stutzman Farms*	100% Natural cellulose Biodegradable 99% Dust-free
Litter Lite (Powder)	*Wysong West*	100% Natural wood pulp Biodegradable Dust-Free
Litter Lite (Powder)	*Wysong West*	100% Natural wood pulp Biodegradable Dust-Free
Neat-N-Sweet Cat Litter (Powder)	*Virginia Mills*	100% Natural Biodegradable Dust-free
PineFresh Cat Litter (Powder)	*Cansorb Industries Corp.*	100% Pine wood Biodegradable Dust-free
Yesterday's News (Powder)	*Eco-Matrix, Inc.*	100% Recycled newspaper Biodegradable Dust-free

CHAPTER 8

The Garage

O f all our possessions, the automobile undoubtedly has the greatest impact on the environment, both in consuming natural resources and releasing pollutants.

- ◆ Production of gasoline for passenger cars uses one of every six barrels of crude oil consumed in the U.S.

- ◆ Americans use one billion gallons of motor oil every year, and at least one-third of it is discarded into the environment.

- ◆ Every year, the average car releases its own weight of carbon dioxide into the atmosphere, contributing to the greenhouse effect.

- ◆ Americans discard an estimated 260 million automobile tires each year, and literally billions of old tires are now clogging landfills.

- ◆ More than half of the 450,000 tons of lead released into the air each year comes from leaded gasoline used in older cars.

- ◆ An estimated 64 million lead-acid batteries from automobiles are discarded each year. Most of them end up in landfills.

- ◆ As many as 9 million automobiles are discarded, with the majority rusting away in junkyards or scarring the landscape.

☞ Automobiles and the Environment

The litany of environmental ills caused by automobiles is seemingly endless. Cars and trucks are the major contributors to air pollution and smog in most cities. Researchers from the University of California calculate that the use of gasoline and diesel fuel causes 30,000 deaths annually from lung and heart disease. The American Lung Association estimates that air pollution caused by cars and trucks, as well as factories and power plants, costs the United States $40 billion each year in lost productivity and health-care costs. Chlorofluorocarbons leaking out of automobile air conditioners are a significant contributor to the destruction of the ozone layer.

Recycled Oil

The disposal of used motor oil is a significant environmental problem. Many do-it-yourselfers either pour used car oil down the drain or into the ground where it can make its way into water supplies. Used oil contains toxins, including lead, cadmium, and polyaromatic hydrocarbons.

Fortunately, motor oil can be recycled—it gets dirty rather than wears out. Recycled oil is clean enough for even high-performance engines.

Some gas stations serve as drop-off centers for motor oil recyclers. Check the service stations in your area. Remember, every gallon of oil recycled helps prevent pollution.

Increased Fuel Economy

It's true that we have seen significant improvements in automobiles in recent years. Average miles per gallon (mpg) in the U.S. grew from 13.1 in 1973 to 17.9 in 1985, a 66 percent increase; for new cars it now hovers around 26 mpg. That increase cut American gasoline consumption by 20 billion gallons per year, reducing oil imports by 1.3 million barrels per day. But there is still substantial room for improvement.

Reformulated and Detergent Gasolines

Some reductions in pollution can be achieved by changing the composition of gasoline, a process called reformulation. This is achieved primarily by removing many of the constituents that vaporize at low temperatures and escape into the atmosphere from the gas tank and the throttle. Refiners also remove some of the complex chemicals, called aromatics and olefins, that often escape through the tailpipe without being burned. Arco Corp. was the first to introduce a reformulated gasoline, replacing in August, 1989, its leaded regular gas distributed in California with an unleaded substitute called EC-1.

EC-1 reduces the emissions from pre-1975 cars by 20 percent. That amount is substantial. Such cars represent only 15 percent of all cars registered in Southern California but they produce 30 percent of automotive pollution. Shell brought out a similar fuel in both regular and premium grades. Conoco, Diamond Shamrock, Exxon, Marathon, Phillips, and Sun have also introduced cleaner fuels in various states.

Another option for motorists is the use of detergent gasolines, readily available at many service stations. These keep your engine running cleaner, and a clearner engine emits less pollutants. This is especially important for engines equipped with fuel injectors.

Decreased Emissions

Significant reductions in polluting emissions have also been achieved in the past 20 years, primarily through catalytic converters, which reduce the emissions of unburned hydrocarbons and nitrogen oxides. Cars emit 34 percent of the nitrogen oxides in our air and 27 percent of the hydrocarbons. But while emissions have been reduced, the number of cars in the country has increased by 50 percent, leading to an increase in smog.

What Government Can Do

A significant change in our use of automobiles will most likely be introduced only by government legislation. The simplest thing for Congress to do would be to increase motor-vehicle efficiency standards to a more reasonable level, something above 30 and perhaps closer to 40 miles per gallon. A stiff tax on gas guzzlers has long been presented as another way to improve fuel economy.

Congress should also mandate reduced emissions from new automobiles, perhaps by such means as requiring research and programs leading to the use of electrically powered cars. Finally, Congress should increase funding for mass transportation systems that would reduce the use of cars.

☞ Elsewhere in the Garage

When cleaning your car, the same considerations apply as elsewhere in the house. Use biodegradable detergents and use the minimum amount necessary. Other car-care products, such as waxes, have no appreciable effect on the environment unless they are thrown away without being used up. Degreasers containing lanolin or similar degradable oils are better for cleaning your hands than gasoline, which irritates your skin and is a pollutant when washed down the drain.

A bicycle is a good investment for the environment if you use it frequently instead of driving your car. It's also good for your heart and lungs.

☞ Green Thinking _____

What You Can Do at Home

No matter what kind of car you have, you can minimize your impact on the environment by a variety of other actions.

DO:

✔ Keep your tires properly inflated; underinflation can rob you of 5 percent of your mileage. It is estimated that 50 to 80 percent of all tires in the U.S. are underinflated.

✔ Use radial tires. They give 3 to 5 percent more fuel economy.

✔ Purchase new tires from a dealer who will recycle your old ones.

✔ Keep your car tuned up. A well-tuned car can use as much as 9 percent less gasoline, and thus produce 9 percent fewer emissions. Also keep the brakes adjusted so they don't drag.

✔ Obey speed limits. You get 20 percent better mileage at 55 mph than at 70 mph.

✔ Patronize air-conditioning repair shops that recycle the chlorofluorocarbon refrigerant.

✔ Make sure your old battery will be recycled rather than thrown in a landfill.

DON'T:

✘ Don't use leaded gasoline in your new car, as an estimated 20 percent of new-car owners do, thereby releasing lead into the air and destroying their catalytic converters.

✘ Don't top off your fuel tank. Spilled gasoline is a major source of air pollution.

✘ Don't carry around extra weight in the car unnecessarily. An extra 100 pounds can reduce miles per gallon by 1 percent for an average car.

☞ Anatomy of a Green Product

Buy the highest mileage automobile that will suit your needs. A stick shift is environmentally preferable to an automatic transmission because it gives better mileage—an automatic transmission typically consumes as much as 15 percent of the engine's power output.

The most environmentally desirable products have the following characteristics:

Motor Oil
Recycled contents and packaging.

Cleaning Products
100 percent natural, biodegradable, phosphate-free, concentrated, recycled and/or recyclable packaging.

Note: At this time, there are very few choices for environmentally conscious motorists, so we have not provided product listings. President's Choice Green Motor Oil is recycled, and is available through Loblaws International grocery stores. Valvoline Motor Oil is not recycled, but is packaged in a recycled plastic container. As for cleaning products, Turtle Wax Zip Car Wash (powder) is biodegradable and phosphate-free, as well as concentrated.

PART II

The Mail-Order Shopper's Guide

Shopping at Home

☞ About the Mail-Order Shopper's Guide

This section provides listing of environmentally sound products that can be obtained through mail-order catalogs, although some can also be found in natural food stores. These products also tend to be made with great concern for the environment, and are therefore among the "greenest" in the book.

The chapters in the section are organized in the same way as those in the first section:

- Laundry
- Kitchen
- Nursery
- Bathroom
- Broom Closet
- Workshop
- Yard and Pet Supplies
- Garage

Each section recaps the main criteria used when selecting green products. (See the corresponding chapters in Part I for background information.) The numbers in the third column (see sample listing below) correspond to the catalogs listed in pages 231 to 236.

Rainwater Herbal Baby Shampoo (Liquid) Nature's Gate/Levlad, Inc.	Biodegradable Vegetable oil base	21, 45, 104

CHAPTER 9

The Laundry

☞ Mail-Order Product Criteria

The most environmentally desirable products have the following characteristics:

Laundry Soaps and Detergents
100 percent natural (no synthetic chemicals, applies only to soaps), phosphate-free, chlorine-free, vegetable oil base, unscented, dye-free, concentrated, recycled and/or recyclable packaging.

Bleaches
Powdered—chlorine-free, recycled packaging, concentrated.

Product/Manufacturer	Description	Catalog

Laundry Soaps and Detergents

Product/Manufacturer	Description	Catalog
Allen's Naturally Laundry Detergent (Liquid) Allen's Naturally	Phosphate-free Chlorine-free Unscented Dye-free Highly concentrated	10, 79, 32
BioSuds Laundry Detergent (Liquid) Biobottoms/Granny's Products	Phosphate-free Chlorine-free Unscented Concentrated	55
Body Shop Bio-Clean (Liquid) The Body Shop/Mark Transfer Co.	100% Natural Phosphate-free Chlorine-free Vegetable oil base Unscented Dye-free	47
Ecco Bella Suds Soap (Liquid) Ecco Bella	Phosphate-free Chlorine-free Concentrated	7
Ecover Laundry Powder (Powder) Mercantile Food Co.	100% Natural Phosphate-free Chlorine-free Vegetable oil base	7, 45, 81
Ecover Liquid Laundry Soap (Liquid) Mercantile Food Co.	100% Natural Phosphate-free Chlorine-free Vegetable oil base	7, 45, 81
Granny's Power Plus (Liquid) Granny's Old Fashioned	Phosphate-free Chlorine-free Unscented Dye-free	1, 32, 77
Life Tree Premium Laundry Soap (Liquid) Sierra Dawn	Phosphate-free Chlorine-free Dye-free	7, 17
Liquid Crystal Baby Laundry (Liquid) Miracel	Phosphate-free Chlorine-free Unscented Dye-free Concentrated	62

Product/Manufacturer	Description	Catalog
Natural Castile Soap (Liquid) Community Soap Factory	100% Natural Phosphate-free Chlorine-free Vegetable oil base Dye-free	10
Neo Life Plus (Powder) Neo Life	Phosphate-free Chlorine-free	8, 38
Neo Life Super Plus (Powder) Neo Life	Low-phosphate Chlorine-free	8, 38
Neway Laundry Compound (Powder) Neway	Chlorine-free Unscented	80
Newliquid Laundry Compound (Liquid) Neway	Phosphate-free Chlorine-free Unscented	80
"Professional" Laundry Compound (Powder) Home Service Products	Chlorine-free Concentrated	4, 17, 48 98
Seventh Generation Laundry Soap (Liquid) Seventh Generation	100% Natural Phosphate-free Chlorine-free Concentrated	81
Winter White Laundry Powder (Powder) Mountain Fresh Products	Phosphate-free Chlorine-free Concentrated	81, 32
Winter White Laundry Soap (Liquid) Mountain Fresh Products	Phosphate-free Chlorine-free Concentrated	81, 32
Winter White Pre-Wash (Liquid) Mountain Fresh Products	Phosphate-free Chlorine-free	4, 32, 81

Bleaches

Ecco Bella Booster & Whitener (Powder) Ecco Bella	Chlorine-free Unscented	7

Product/Manufacturer	Description	Catalog
Newbrite Bleach **(Powder)** Neway	Chlorine-free	80
"Professional" Bleach **(Powder)** Home Service Products	Chlorine-free Concentrated	4, 17, 48 98
Seventh Generation Liquid **Bleach (Liquid)** Seventh Generation	Chlorine-free Concentrated	81
Winter White Bleach **(Liquid)** Mountain Fresh Products	Chlorine-free Concentrated	4, 17

Miscellaneous Laundry Products

Product/Manufacturer	Description	Catalog
Allen's Naturally **Fabric Soft (Liquid)** Allen's Naturally	Phosphate-free Chlorine-free Unscented Dye-free Concentrated	8, 10, 23 79
Ecover Fabric **Conditioner (Liquid)** Mercantile Food Co.	100% Natural Phosphate-free Chlorine-free Vegetable oil base	7, 45, 81
Ecover Wool Wash **(Liquid)** Mercantile Food Co.	100% Natural Phosphate-free Chlorine-free Vegetable oil base	7, 45, 81
Golden Lotus **Soft-n-Fresh (Liquid)** Mountain Fresh Products	Phosphate-free Chlorine-free Concentrated	32, 81
"Professional" Fabric **Softener (Liquid)** Home Service Products	Phosphate-free Chlorine-free Concentrated	4, 17, 48 98

CHAPTER 10

The Kitchen

☞ Mail-Order Product Criteria

The most environmentally desirable products have the following characteristics:

Food Contents
Organic (pesticide-free), additive-free, preservative-free, no tropical oils, no or low sugar, recycled/recyclable/resuable packaging.

Paper Goods
100 percent recycled or natural fibers, biodegradable, dioxin-free (unbleached or oxygen-bleached), undyed (or if dyed, only light colors or prints), unscented.

Cleaning products
Biodegradable, phosphate-free, chlorine-free, vegetable oil base, unscented, dye-free, recycled and/or recyclable packaging.

Product/Manufacturer	Description	Catalog

Kitchen Paper Products

Product/Manufacturer	Description	Catalog
Canvas Tote Bags (Cotton) L.L. Bean	100% Natural fiber Biodegradable Reusable	133
Cellophane/Cellulose Bags (Paper) Seventh Generation	100% Biodegradable Recyclable/reusable	1, 4, 7 8, 10, 32 34, 41, 45 81
Cotton String Shopping Bags (Cotton) Seventh Generation	100% Natural fiber Biodegradable Reusable	81
Drawstring Shopping Bags (Cotton) Gardener's Supply	100% Natural fiber Biodegradable Reusable	86
Eco-Filter Coffee Filter (Cotton) Eco-Filter Products	100% Natural fiber Biodegradable Reusable/recyclable	7, 81
Lola Bottle & Dish Brush (Vegetable Fiber/Wood) Lola	100% Natural fiber Biodegradable Reusable/recyclable	7, 45
Natural Brew Coffee Filters (Paper) Rockline, Inc.	Biodegradable Unbleached	81
Picnic "China" Dinner Plates (Paper) Seventh Generation	100% Recycled paper Biodegradable	81
Picnic "China" Salad Plates (Paper) Seventh Generation	100% Recycled paper Biodegradable	81
Picnic "China" Soup Bowls (Paper) Seventh Generation	100% Recycled paper Biodegradable	81
Save-a-Tree Shopping Bags (Cotton) Save-a-Tree	100% Natural fiber Biodegradable Reusable	131
TreeSavers Shopping Bags (Cotton) TreeSavers	100% Natural fiber Biodegradable Reusable	132

Product/Manufacturer	Description	Catalog
Vegetable Fiber Scrub Brush (Vegetable Fiber) Kuroshio	100% Natural fiber Biodegradable Reusable/recyclable	7, 45

Trash Bags

Product/Manufacturer	Description	Catalog
Heavy Duty Paper Garbage Bags (Paper) Set Point, Inc.	100% Biodegradable Available in gallon sizes Recyclable	81, 118 30, 13, & 8
Paper Trash Bags (Paper) Stone Container	100% Biodegradable Recyclable/reusable	81, 118

Kitchen Cleansers

Product/Manufacturer	Description	Catalog
Allen's Dish Soap (Liquid) Allen's Naturally	Phosphate-free Chlorine-free Unscented Dye-free	4, 8, 10 32, 79
Allen's Dishwasher Detergent (Powder) Allen's Naturally	Chlorine-free Unscented Dye-free	4, 8, 10 32, 79
Ecover Dishwashing Soap (Liquid) Mercantile Food Co.	100% Natural Phosphate-free Chlorine-free Vegetable oil base	7, 45, 81 118
Granny's Aloe Care Dish Soap (Liquid) Granny's Old Fashioned	Phosphate-free Chlorine-free Unscented Dye-free	1, 32, 77
Kleer Dish Detergent (Liquid) Mountain Fresh Products	Phosphate-free Chlorine-free Dye-free Concentrated	4, 17, 32, 104
Kleer II Dishwasher Gel (Liquid) Mountain Fresh Products	Phosphate-free Concentrated	4, 17

The Kitchen

Product/Manufacturer	Description	Catalog
Life Tree Premium Dish Soap (Liquid) Sierra Dawn	Phosphate-free Chlorine-free	7, 17
Mellow Yellow Dishwashing Soap (Liquid) Neo Life	Phosphate-free	8, 38
Neo Life Auto Dishwashing Powder (Powder) Neo Life	Low-phosphate Dye-free Concentrated	8, 38
"Professional" Auto Dishwasher (Powder) Home Service Products	Phosphate-free Chlorine-free Concentrated	4, 17, 48 98
Seventh Generation Dishwasher Gel (Liquid) Seventh Generation	Phosphate-free	81
Seventh Generation Dishwashing Soap (Liquid) Seventh Generation	100% Natural Phosphate-free	81

Hot Cereals

Walnut Acres Hot Cereals Walnut Acres	Organic ingredients No artificial additives No preservatives Paper packaging	118

Miscellaneous Breakfast Foods

Walnut Acres Pancake Mixes Walnut Acres	Organic ingredients No artificial additives No preservatives Paper packaging	118

Product/Manufacturer	Description	Catalog

Juices

Walnut Acres Vegetable Juice Walnut Acres	Organic ingredients No artificial additives No preservatives	118

Condiments

Walnut Acres Mayonnaise Walnut Acres	Organic ingredients No artificial additives No preservatives Glass packaging	118

Pasta and Sauces

Walnut Acres Marinara Sauce Walnut Acres	Organic ingredients No artificial additives No preservatives	118
Walnut Acres Whole Wheat Pasta Walnut Acres	100% Organic ingredients No artificial additives No preservatives	118

The
Kitchen

CHAPTER 11

The Nursery

☞ Mail-Order Product Criteria

The most environmentally desirable products have the following characteristics:

Diapers
Multiple-use is best: natural fibers.
Single use: 100 percent biodegradable material.

Baby-care products
100 percent natural (no synthetic chemicals), biodegradable, vegetable oil base, talc-free unscented, dye-free, recycled and/or recyclable packaging.

Nipples
Nitrosamine-free or low nitrosamine.

Bottles
Recyclable or reusable.

Product/Manufacturer	Description	Catalog

Diapers

Product/Manufacturer	Description	Catalog
Biobottoms Diaper Covers (Wool or Cotton) Biobottoms	Natural fiber Biodegradable Reusable/recyclable	55
Bumkins Cloth Diapers (100% Cotton w/ Shell) Bumkins Family Products	Natural fiber Waterproof shell Reusable/recyclable	94
Cotton Cloud Diapers (100% Cotton) Baby Bunz & Co.	Natural fiber Biodegradable Reusable/recyclable	54
Cuddlers Cloth Diapers (100% Cotton) Cuddlers Cloth Diapers	100% Cotton with Velcro Biodegradable Reusable/recyclable	56, 60
Dappi Diaper Cover (Cotton Blend) TL Care	Reusable/recyclable	96
Diaperaps Diaper Covers (Cotton Blend) Diaperaps	Reusable/recyclable	95
Dovetails Diapers (Paper, Single-Use) Family Clubhouse	100% Biodegradable Chemical-free Plastic-free Use with diaper cover	53, 54, 58 63, 67, 70 71
HappiNappi Diapers (100% Cotton) Baby Bunz & Co.	Natural fiber Biodegradable Reusable/recyclable	54
Nikky's Diaper Covers (Wool or Cotton) Nikky's	Natural fiber Reusable/recyclable	53, 54, 58 62, 64, 65 66, 67, 72 74
Portland Soakers Diaper Cover (Wool) Portland Soakers	Natural fiber Reusable/recyclable	68
Rainbow Diapers (100% Cotton) Natural Baby Co.	Natural fiber Reusable/recyclable	54, 62, 63 66
Rubber Duckies Diaper Covers (Nylon) The R. Duck Co.	Reusable/recyclable	93, 97

Product/Manufacturer	Description	Catalog
Wrap Ups Diaper Covers (Nylon) The R. Duck Co.	Reusable/recyclable	93, 97

Baby-Care Products

Product/Manufacturer	Description	Catalog
Aubrey Natural Baby Bath Soap (Liquid) Aubrey Organics	100% Natural Biodegradable Vegetable oil base	3, 6, 19
Aubrey Natural Baby Lotion (Liquid) Aubrey Organics	100% Natural Biodegradable Vegetable oil base	3, 6, 19
Aubrey Natural Baby Shampoo (Liquid) Aubrey Organics	100% Natural Biodegradable Vegetable oil base	1, 3, 6 19
Autumn Harp Extra Mild Baby Shampoo (Liquid) Autumn Harp, Inc.	100% Natural Biodegradable Vegetable oil base	6, 9, 17 21, 93
Baby Massage Baby Lotion (Liquid) Mountain Fresh Products	Biodegradable Vegetable oil base Unscented Dye-free	62
Baby Massage Oil (Liquid) Mountain Fresh Products	100% Natural Biodegradable Vegetable oil base Dye-free	62
Baby Massage Tearless Shampoo (Liquid) Mountain Fresh Products	Biodegradable Unscented Dye-free	62
Baby Massage Tearless Wash (Liquid) Mountain Fresh Products	Biodegradable Unscented Dye-free	62
Baby Mild & Kind Care Cream (Liquid) Borlind's of Germany	Biodegradable Vegetable oil base	76
Baby Mild & Kind Child's Bath (Liquid) Borlind's of Germany	Biodegradable Vegetable oil base	76

The
Nursery

Product/Manufacturer	Description	Catalog
Baby Mild & Kind Shampoo (Liquid) Borlind's of Germany	Biodegradable Vegetable oil base	76
Calendula Baby Cream (Cream) Weleda	100% Natural Biodegradable Vegetable oil base	1, 17, 18 19, 20, 21 70, 74, 93
Calendula Baby Oil (Liquid) Weleda	100% Natural Biodegradable Vegetable oil base	1, 6, 9 18, 19, 58 70, 74, 93
Calendula Baby Soap (Bar) Weleda	100% Natural Biodegradable Vegetable oil base	1, 6, 9 18, 19, 43 58, 70, 74
Camomile Baby Cream (Cream) Lindos	100% Natural Biodegradable Vegetable oil base	1, 14
Camomile Baby Oil (Liquid) Lindos	100% Natural Biodegradable Vegetable oil base	1, 14
Camomile Baby Soap (Bar) Lindos	100% Natural Biodegradable Vegetable oil base	1, 14
Canada's Babycakes Soap (Bar) All Natural Soap, Inc.	100% Natural Biodegradable Vegetable oil base Recycled paper	81
Chicks Baby Lotion (Liquid) Jason Natural Products	Biodegradable Vegetable oil base	11
Chicks Bubble Bath (Liquid) Jason Natural Products	Biodegradable Vegetable oil base	11
Chicks Tearless Baby Shampoo (Liquid) Jason Natural Products	Biodegradable Vegetable oil base	11
Country Comfort Baby Cream (Cream) Country Comfort	100% Natural Biodegradable Vegetable oil base	1, 21, 93

Product/Manufacturer	Description	Catalog
Country Comfort Baby Oil (Liquid) Country Comfort	100% Natural Biodegradable Vegetable oil base	1, 21, 93
Country Comfort Baby Powder (Powder) Country Comfort	100% Natural Biodegradable Talc-free	1, 21, 93
Earthchild Baby Oil (Liquid) Autumn Harp, Inc.	100% Natural Biodegradable Vegetable oil base	6, 9, 17 21, 75, 81 93
Gently Yours Tearless Shampoo (Liquid) Granny's Old Fashioned	Biodegradable Vegetable oil base Unscented Dye-free	1, 32, 41 77
Lavender Baby Soap (Bar) Under the Apple Tree	100% Natural Biodegradable Vegetable oil base	19
Lavender/Calendula Baby Oil (Liquid) Lakon Herbals	Organic herbs and oils Biodegradable Vegetable oil base	124
Loanda Lavender Baby Soap (Bar) Carme, Inc.	100% Natural Biodegradable Vegetable oil base	9, 21
Natural Baby Shampoo (Liquid) Under the Apple Tree	100% Natural Biodegradable Vegetable oil base	19
Rainwater Herbal Baby Shampoo (Liquid) Nature's Gate/Levlad, Inc.	Biodegradable Vegetable oil base	21, 45, 104
Royale Baby Bath (Liquid) Royale Renaissance	Dye-free Concentrated	121
Royale Baby Lotion (Liquid) Royale Renaissance	Dye-free Concentrated	121
Royale Baby Powder (Powder) Royale Renaissance	Talc-free Dye-free Concentrated	121

The Nursery

Product/Manufacturer	Description	Catalog
Royale Baby Shampoo (Liquid) Royale Renaissance	Dye-free Concentrated	121
Royale Herbal Bath (Liquid) Royale Renaissance	Dye-free Concentrated	121
Seventh Generation Baby Wipes (Paper) Seventh Generation	Biodegradable 33% Cotton fiber Dioxin-free paper	81
Supermild Baby Castile Soap (Liquid) All-One-God-Faith, Inc.	100% Natural Biodegradable Vegetable oil base	21, 45
Talc-Free Baby Powder (Powder) Autumn Harp, Inc.	100% Natural Biodegradable Talc-free	6, 17, 21 75, 81, 93
Tom's Honeysuckle Baby Shampoo (Liquid) Tom's of Maine	100% Natural Biodegradable Vegetable oil base	21, 81
Un-Petroleum Jelly (Cream) Autumn Harp, Inc.	100% Natural Biodegradable Vegetable oil base	6, 17, 21 75, 81, 93
Vegelatum (Cream) Mountain Fresh Products	Biodegradable Vegetable oil base Unscented Dye-free	62

CHAPTER 12

The Bathroom

☞ Mail-Order Product Criteria

The most environmentally desirable products have the following characteristics:

Paper Goods
Recycled or natural fibers, biodegradable, dioxin-free (unbleached or oxygen-bleached), undyed (or if dyed, only light colors or prints), unscented.

Soaps, Dental Products, Body and Skin, Hair Care, Sun-Tanning Products, Deodorants, Shaving Products
100 percent natural (no synthetic chemicals), biodegradable, vegetable oil based, talc-free (body powders), unscented, dye-free, non-aerosol, recycled, recyclable, or reusable packaging.

Feminine Hygiene and Cosmetics
100 percent natural (no synthetic chemicals), biodegradable, vegetable oil base, unscented, dye-free. Tampons: applicator-free or biodegradable applicator, unscented.

Product/Manufacturer	Description	Catalog

Soaps

Product/Manufacturer	Description	Catalog
African Bio-Botanica Soap (Liquid) African Bio-Botanica, Inc.	Biodegradable Vegetable oil base	7
Alexandra Avery Soaps (Bar) Alexandra Avery	100% Natural Biodegradable Vegetable oil base	9, 17, 111
Apiana Soaps (Bar) Bienen Mathys	Biodegradable Vegetable oil base	9, 106
Aubrey Soaps (Bar) Aubrey Organics	100% Natural Biodegradable Vegetable oil base	3, 7, 9 45
Body Shop Soaps (Bar) The Body Shop/Mark Transfer Co.	100% Natural Biodegradable Vegetable oil base	47
Chandrika Ayurvedic Soap (Bar) Auromere	100% Natural Biodegradble Vegetable oil base	9, 21, 104 128
Chef's Soap (Bar) The Living Source	Biodegradable Vegetable oil base Unscented Dye-free	38
Clearly Natural Glycerine Soap (Bar) Clearly Natural	Biodegradable Vegetable oil base Unscented/scented	4, 9, 21 51, 104
Desert Essence Castile Soap (Liquid) Desert Essence	Biodegradable Vegetable oil base	7, 21
French Soap (Bar) Janice Corp.	Biodegradable Unscented Dye-free	10
Golden Lotus Soaps (Liquid) Mountain Fresh Products	Biodegradable Vegetable oil base	4, 22
Gregory Aromatic Soaps (Bar) C.A. Gregory Aromatics, Ltd.	100% Natural Biodegradable Vegetable oil base	9, 106

Product/Manufacturer	Description	Catalog
Heavenly Soap Natural Soaps (Bar) Heavenly Soap	100% Natural Biodegradable Vegetable oil base	114
Jason Natural Soaps (Liquid) Jason Natural Products	Biodegradable Vegetable oil base	11
Kiss My Face Olive Oil Soap (Bar) Kiss My Face Corp.	100% Natural Biodegradable Vegetable oil base	7, 9, 21 117
Kiss My Face Pure Olive Oil Soap (Bar) Kiss My Face Corp.	100% Natural Biodegradable Vegetable oil base Unscented	7, 9, 21 117
Lavenos Hand Soap (Liquid) Livos PlantChemistry	100% Natural Biodegradable Vegetable oil base Unscented Dye-free	24, 45, 46
McClinton's Barilla Soaps (Bar) E. McCormack & Co.	100% Natural Biodegradable Vegetable oil base Dye-free	9, 106
Naturade Aloe Vera 80 Soap (Liquid) Naturade Products	Biodegradable Vegetable oil base	4, 21
Natural Castile Soaps (Liquid) Community Soap Factory	100% Natural Biodegradable Vegetable oil base	9, 45, 104
Nature de France Soaps (Bar) Nature de France, Inc.	100% Natural Biodegradable Vegetable oil base	19
Olivea Greek Olive Oil Soap (Bar) Olivea	100% Natural Biodegradable Vegetable oil base	9
Orjene Soaps (Bar) Orjene Natural Cosmetics	Biodegradable Vegetable oil base	5, 6

The Bath-room

Product/Manufacturer	Description	Catalog
Pacifica Soaps (Bar) Philippine Herbal Group	100% Natural Biodegradable Vegetable oil base Dye-free	9, 106
Phebo Soaps (Bar) Parfumarias Phebo	100% Natural Biodegradable Vegetable oil base	9, 106
Real Aloe Vera Soap (Bar) The Real Aloe Co.	Biodegradable Vegetable oil base	7, 115
Sappo Hill Soaps (Bar) Sappo Hill Soapworks	100% Natural Biodegradable Vegetable oil base Available dye-free Available unscented	4
Simmons Pure Vegetarian Soaps (Bar) Simmons Handcrafts	100% Natural Biodegradable Vegetable oil base	113
Simple Soaps (Bar) Simple Products	Biodegradable Vegetable oil base Unscented Dye-free	10, 38
Sirena Soaps (Liquid) Sirena Products	Biodegradable Vegetable oil base Unscented Dye-free	10
Tea Tree Oil Soaps (Bar) Thursday Plantation Products	Biodegradable Vegetable oil base	9
The Body Shop Soaps (Bar) The Body Shop, Inc.	Biodegradable Vegetable oil base	127
Under the Apple Tree Soaps (Bar) Under the Apple Tree	Biodegradable Vegetable oil base	19
Walter Rau Fine Soaps (Bar) Walter Rau Company	100% Natural Biodegradable Vegetable oil base	14

Product/Manufacturer	Description	Catalog
Weleda Soaps (Bar) Weleda	100% Natural Biodegradable Vegetable oil base	2, 5, 9 14, 17, 18 19, 20, 21

Dental Products

Product/Manufacturer	Description	Catalog
Dentagrin Tooth Gel (Gel) 4-D Hobe, Inc.	100% Natural Biodegradable Vegetable oil base	120
Denti-Care (Powder) African Bio-Botanica, Inc.	Biodegradable Vegetable oil base	7
Dentie Toothpaste (Paste) Muso Co., Ltd.	100% Natural Biodegradable Vegetable oil base	9
Desert Essence Dental Floss (Waxed) Desert Essence	Vegetable oil base Dye-free	7, 21
Desert Essence Mouthwash (Liquid) Desert Essence	Biodegradable Vegetable oil base	7, 21
Homeodent Toothpaste (Paste) Boiron/Borneman, Inc.	Biodegradable Vegetable oil base Dye-free	21
IPSAB Herbal Gum Treatment (Powder) Heritage Products	100% Natural Biodegradable	9
IPSAB Tooth Powder (Powder) Heritage Products	100% Natural Biodegradable	9
Ipsadent Herbal Mouthwash (Liquid) Heritage Products	100% Natural Biodegradable Vegetable oil base	9
Mer-Flu-an Tooth Powder (Powder) American Merfluan, Inc.	100% Natural Biodegradable	9, 51

The Bath-room

Product/Manufacturer	Description	Catalog
Natural Gum Toothpaste (Paste) Desert Essence	Biodegradable Vegetable oil base Dye-free	7, 21
Natural Mint Mouthwash (Liquid) Aubrey Organics	100% Natural Biodegradable Vegetable oil base	3, 7, 9 45
Nature de France Toothpaste (Paste) Nature de France, Inc.	100% Natural Biodegradable Vegetable oil base	19
Nature's Gate Mouthwashes (Liquid) Nature's Gate/Levlad, Inc.	Biodegradable Vegetable oil base	21, 45, 104
Nature's Gate Toothpastes (Paste) Nature's Gate/Levlad, Inc.	Biodegradable Vegetable oil base	21, 45, 104
Paro Dent'Or Toothpaste (Paste) Voerman Laboratories	100% Natural Biodegradable	9, 106
Peelu Tooth Powder (Powder) Peelu Products	Biodegradable Dye-free	21
Peelu Toothpaste (Paste) Peelu Products	Biodegradable Vegetable oil base Dye-free	21
Rainbow Natural Mint Toothpast (Paste) Rainbow Research Corp.	Biodegradable Vegetable oil base Dye-free	104, 116
Tom's Natural Flossing Ribbon Tom's of Maine	Recycled paper package	2, 4, 7 9, 21
Tom's Natural Mouthwash (Liquid) Tom's of Maine	100% Natural Biodegradable Vegetable oil base	2, 4, 7 9, 21
Tom's Natural Toothpastes (Paste) Tom's of Maine	100% Natural Biodegradable Vegetable oil base Recycled paper Recyclable aluminum tube	2, 4, 7 9, 21

Product/Manufacturer	Description	Catalog
Vicco Herbal Toothpaste (Paste) Auromere	Biodegradable Vegetable oil base	21, 28, 45
Weleda Mouthwash Concentrate (Liquid) Weleda	100% Natural Biodegradable Concentrated	2, 5, 9 14, 17, 18 19, 20, 21
Weleda Toothpastes (Paste) Weleda	100% Natural Biodegradable Vegetable oil base	2, 5, 9 14, 17, 18 19, 20, 21

Body and Skin Products

Abracadabra Clays (Powder) Abracadabra, Inc.	100% Natural Biodegradable	19
Acne-Care (Cream) African Bio-Botanica, Inc.	Biodegradable Vegetable oil base	7
African Bio-Botanica Lotions (Liquid) African Bio-Botanica, Inc.	Biodegradable Vegetable oil base	7
Alba Botanica Lotions (Liquid) Alba Botanica Cosmetics	Biodegradable Vegetable oil base	9, 17, 112
Alexandra Avery Creams (Liquid) Alexandra Avery	Biodegradable Vegetable oil base	9, 111
Alexandra Avery Lip Balms (Cream) Alexandra Avery	Biodegradable Vegetable oil base	9, 111
Almond Sun Cleanser/Mask (Cream) Gemma Abhoud	100% Natural Biodegradable Vegetable oil base Dye-free	9
Aloegen Skin Emulsions (Liquid) Aloegen Natural Products	Biodegradable Vegetable oil base	130

The Bath-room

Product/Manufacturer	Description	Catalog
Amazing Grains Cleanser (Powder) Body Love Natural Cosmetics	100% Natural Biodegradable Dye-free Concentrated	9
Analgesic Achillea Liniment (Liquid) Lakon Herbals	Organic herbs and oils Biodegradable Vegetable oil base Glass packaging	124
Apache Gold Skin Care Products (Cream) 4-D Hobe, Inc.	100% Natural Biodegradable Vegetable oil base	120
Apiana Honey Lotions & Creams (Liquid) Bienen Mathys	Biodegradable Vegetable oil base	9, 106
Aqualin Oil Free Moisturizer (Liquid) Hlavin Cosmetics	100% Natural Biodegradable Vegetable oil base	4, 9, 21
Aubrey Facial Products (Liquid) Aubrey Organics	100% Natural Biodegradable Vegetable oil base	3, 7, 9 45
Aura Cacia Body Powders (Powder) Aura Cacia, Inc.	100% Natural Biodegradable Talc-free	2, 9, 51
Autumn Harp Aloe Rose Body Lot (Liquid) Autumn Harp, Inc.	100% Natural Biodegradable Vegetable oil base	6, 9, 17 21, 93
Bindi Herbal Cleanser (Liquid) Bindi Cosmetics, Inc.	100% Natural Biodegradable Vegetable oil base	9
Bindi Moisturizing Cream (Liquid) Bindi Cosmetics, Inc.	100% Natural Biodegradable Vegetable oil base	9
Body Shop Beauty Grains (Powder) The Body Shop/Mark Transfer Co.	100% Natural Biodegradable Unscented/scented Dye-free	47
Body Shop Dusting Powder (Powder) The Body Shop/Mark Transfer Co.	100% Natural Biodegradable Talc-free Dye-free	47

Product/Manufacturer	Description	Catalog
Cleansing Milks (Liquid) Paul Penders Products	Biodegradable Vegetable oil base	4, 9, 17
Cloudworks Rose Cream (Cream) Cloudworks, Inc.	100% Natural Biodegradable Vegetable oil base	9
Comfrey Herbal Salve (Cream) Lakon Herbals	Organic herbs and oils Biodegradable Vegetable oil base	124
Desert Essence Tea Tree Oil (Liquid) Desert Essence	100% Natural Biodegradable Vegetable oil base	7, 21
Earth Science Facial Cleansers (Liquid) Earth Science, Inc.	Biodegradable Vegetable oil base	51, 126
Ecco Bella Body Powders (Powder) Ecco Bella	100% Natural Biodegradable Talc-free	7
Ecco Bella Cleansing Grains (Powder) Ecco Bella	100% Natural Biodegradable	7
Ecco Bella Moisture Lotion (Liquid) Ecco Bella	100% Natural Biodegradable Vegetable oil base	7
Facial Cleansers (Liquid) Under the Apple Tree	Biodegradable Vegetable oil base	19
Green Gold Herbal Salve (Cream) Cloudworks, Inc.	100% Natural Biodegradable Vegetable oil base Dye-free	9
Gregory Aromatic Skin Oils (Liquid) C.A. Gregory Aromatics, Ltd.	100% Natural Biodegradable Vegetable oil base	9, 106
Heavenly Soap Herbal Salve (Cream) Heavenly Soap	100% Natural Biodegradable Vegetable oil base	114

The Bath-room

Product/Manufacturer	Description	Catalog
Jason Natural Body Lotions (Liquid) Jason Natural Products	Biodegradable Vegetable oil base	11
Jurlique Cleansing Lotion (Liquid) Jurlique/D'Namis, Ltd.	Organic herbs 100% Natural Biodegradable Vegetable oil base Unscented Dye-free	125
Jurlique Skin Conditioners (Liquid) Jurlique/D'Namis, Ltd.	Organic herbs 100% Natural Biodegradable Vegetable oil base Unscented Dye-free	125
Kiss My Face Moisturizers (Liquid) Kiss My Face Corp.	Biodegradable Vegetable oil base	7, 9, 21 117
Magick Mud Facial Masque (Cream) Magick Botanicals	100% Natural Biodegradable Vegetable oil base Dye-free Concentrated	9
Moisture Guard Lotion (Liquid) Granny's Old Fashioned	Biodegradable Vegetable oil base Unscented Dye-free	1, 32, 41 77
Monoi Bath & Shower Gel (Liquid) Monoi, Inc.	100% Natural Biodegradable Vegetable oil base	9
Monoi Moisturizing Fluid (Liquid) Monoi, Inc.	100% Natural Biodegradable Vegetable oil base	9
Moonsilk Body Powder (Powder) Alexandra Avery	100% Natural Biodegradable Talc-free	9, 111
Paul Penders Creams & Lotions (Cream) Paul Penders Products	Biodegradable Vegetable oil base	4, 9, 17

Product/Manufacturer	Description	Catalog
Real Aloe Burn Spray (Liquid) The Real Aloe Co.	Biodegradable Vegetable oil base	7, 115
Real Aloe Vera Gel & Juice (Liquid) The Real Aloe Co.	100% Natural Biodegradable Vegetable oil base	7, 115
Simple Body Lotion (Liquid) Simple Products	Biodegradable Vegetable oil base Unscented Dye-free	10, 38
Sombra Facial Scrubs & Masks (Cream) Sombra Cosmetics, Inc.	Biodegradable Vegetable oil base	7, 40, 119
Soothing Herbal Blemish Treatment (Liquid) Lakon Herbals	Organic herbs and oils Biodegradable Vegetable oil base Glass packaging	124
Speick Lotions & Creams (Liquid) Walter Rau Company	100% Natural Biodegradable Vegetable oil base	14
Tea Tree Dermol Acne Lotion (Liquid) Thursday Plantation Products	Biodegradable Vegetable oil base	9
Teen Skin Herbal Cleansing Pad (Pads) 4-D Hobe, Inc.	100% Natural Biodegradable Vegetable oil base	120
Terra Flora Body Powder (Powder) Terra Flora, Inc.	100% Natural Biodegradable Talc-free	9, 18
The Body Shop Body Lotions (Liquid) The Body Shop, Inc.	Biodegradable Vegetable oil base	127
The Body Shop Facial Cleansers (Liquid) The Body Shop, Inc.	Biodegradable Vegetable oil base	127
Under the Apple Tree Body Powd (Powder) Under the Apple Tree	100% Natural Biodegradable Talc-free	19

The Bath-room

Product/Manufacturer	Description	Catalog
Under the Apple Tree Lotions (Liquid) Under the Apple Tree	Biodegradable Vegetable oil base Unscented	19
Unscented Bubble Bath (Liquid) Under the Apple Tree	Biodegradable Vegetable oil base Unscented	19
Walnut Acres Natural Soap (Bar) Walnut Acres	100% Natural Biodegradable Dye-free	118
Weleda Lotions & Creams (Liquid) Weleda	100% Natural Biodegradable Vegetable oil base	2, 5, 9 14, 17, 18 19, 20, 21
Wysong Dermal Skin Care (Liquid) Wysong Corp.	Biodegradable Vegetable oil base	7

Hair-Care Products

Product/Manufacturer	Description	Catalog
4-D Hobe Shampoos (Liquid) 4-D Hobe, Inc.	Biodegradable Vegetable oil base	120
African Bio-Botanica Shampoos (Liquid) African Bio-Botanica, Inc.	Biodegradable Vegetable oil base	7
Aloegen Hair Spray (Liquid) Aloegen Natural Products	Biodegradable Vegetable oil base	130
Aubrey Hair Conditioners (Liquid) Aubrey Organics	100% Natural Biodegradable Vegetable oil base	3, 7, 9 45
Aubrey Hair Highliter Mousses (Liquid) Aubrey Organics	100% Natural Biodegradable Vegetable oil base	3, 7, 9 45
Aubrey Herbal Shampoos (Liquid) Aubrey Organics	100% Natural Biodegradable Vegetable oil base	3, 7, 9 45
Biogenic Conditioners (Liquid) Aloegen Natural Products	Biodegradable Vegetable oil base	130

Product/Manufacturer	Description	Catalog
Biogenic Treatment Shampoo (Liquid) Aloegen Natural Products	Biodegradable Vegetable oil base	130
Body Shop Hair Spray (Liquid) The Body Shop/Mark Transfer Co.	Biodegradable Vegetable oil base Unscented Dye-free	47
Body Shop Shampoos (Liquid) The Body Shop/Mark Transfer Co.	Biodegradable Vegetable oil base Unscented/scented Dye-free	47
Body Shop Styling Gel (Liquid) The Body Shop/Mark Transfer Co.	Biodegradable Vegetable oil base Dye-free	47
Dr. Hauschka Neem Hair Lotion (Liquid) Dr. Hauschka Cosmetics, Inc.	100% Natural Biodegradable Vegetable oil base	1, 9, 14
Earth Science Hair Spray (Liquid) Earth Science, Inc.	Biodegradable Vegetable oil base	126
Earth Science Mousse (Liquid) Earth Science, Inc.	Biodegradable Vegetable oil base	126
Earth Science Shampoos (Liquid) Earth Science, Inc.	Biodegradable Vegetable oil base	126
Ferm-Hold Hair Spray (Liquid) 4-D Hobe, Inc.	Biodegradable Vegetable oil base CFC-Free	120
Golden Lotus Hair Conditioners (Liquid) Mountain Fresh Products	Biodegradable Vegetable oil base	4, 22
Golden Lotus Shampoos (Liquid) Mountain Fresh Products	Biodegradable Vegetable oil base	4, 22
Herbal Shampoos (Liquid) Community Soap Factory	Biodegradable Vegetable oil base	9, 45, 104

The Bath-room

Product/Manufacturer	Description	Catalog
J.R. Liggett's Bar Shampoo (Bar) J.R. Liggett, Ltd.	100% Natural Biodegradable Vegetable oil base Concentrated Recyclable paper packaging	9, 81
Jason Natural Conditioners (Liquid) Jason Natural Products	Biodegradable Vegetable oil base	11
Jason Natural Shampoos (Liquid) Jason Natural Products	Biodegradable Vegetable oil base	11
Jojoba Nutrient Conditioner (Liquid) Desert Essence	Biodegradable Vegetable oil base	7, 21
Jojoba Spirulina Shampoo (Liquid) Desert Essence	Biodegradable Vegetable oil base	7, 21
Kiss My Face Shampoos (Liquid) Kiss My Face Corp.	Biodegradable Vegetable oil base	7, 9, 21 117
Light Touch Henna (Powder) Lotus Light, Inc.	100% Natural Biodegradable	9
Natural Hairsprays (Liquid) Aubrey Organics	100% Natural Biodegradable Vegetable oil base	3, 7, 9 45
Orjene Shampoos (Liquid) Orjene Natural Cosmetics	Biodegradable Vegetable oil base	5, 6
Rainbow Henna (Powder) Rainbow Research Corp.	Biodegradable Vegetable oil base	104, 116
Rainbow Henna Conditioner (Liquid) Rainbow Research Corp.	Biodegradable Vegetable oil base	104, 116
Rainbow Henna Shampoo (Liquid) Rainbow Research Corp.	Biodegradable Vegetable oil base	104, 116

Product/Manufacturer	Description	Catalog
Rainwater Herbal Shampoos (Liquid) Nature's Gate/Levlad, Inc.	Biodegradable Vegetable oil base	21, 45, 104
Real Aloe Vera Shampoo (Bar) The Real Aloe Co.	Biodegradable Vegetable oil base	7, 115
Simple Shampoo (Liquid) Simple Products	Biodegradable Vegetable oil base Unscented Dye-free	10, 38
Speick Hair Shampoo (Liquid) Walter Rau Company	100% Natural Biodegradable Vegetable oil base	14
Tea Tree Hair Conditioner (Liquid) Thursday Plantation Products	Biodegradable Vegetable oil base	9
Tea Tree Shampoos (Liquid) Thursday Plantation Products	Biodegradable Vegetable oil base	9
The Body Shop Shampoos (Liquid) The Body Shop, Inc.	Biodegradable Vegetable oil base	127
Under the Apple Tree Conditioners (Liquid) Under the Apple Tree	Biodegradable Vegetable oil base	19
Under the Apple Tree Shampoos (Liquid) Under the Apple Tree	Biodegradable Vegetable oil base Concentrated	19
VitaWave Hair Perms (Liquid) VitaWave Products	100% Natural Biodegradable Vegetable oil base	6, 7, 13 17
VitaWave Hair Spray (Liquid) VitaWave Products	Biodegradable Vegetable oil base Dye-free	6, 7, 13 17
VitaWave Herbal Shampoos (Liquid) VitaWave Products	Biodegradable Vegetable oil base Dye-free	6, 7, 13 17

The Bath-room

Product/Manufacturer	Description	Catalog
Weleda Hair Conditioners (Liquid) Weleda	100% Natural Biodegradable Vegetable oil base	2, 5, 9 14, 17, 18 19, 20, 21
Weleda Shampoos (Liquid) Weleda	100% Natural Biodegradable Vegetable oil base Concentrated	2, 5, 9 14, 17, 18 19, 20, 21
Wysong Hair Conditioners (Liquid) Wysong Corp.	100% Natural Biodegradable Vegetable oil base	7
Wysong Natural Shampoos (Liquid) Wysong Corp.	100% Natural Biodegradable Vegetable oil base	7

Sun-Tanning Products

4-D Suntan Lotions & Oils (Liquid) 4-D Hobe, Inc.	Biodegradable Vegetable oil base	120
Aloe Gardenia Sun Oil (Liquid) Alexandra Avery	100% Natural Biodegradable Vegetable oil base	9, 111
Aura Cacia Sun Butter (Cream) Aura Cacia, Inc.	100% Natural Biodegradable Vegetable oil base	2, 9, 17
Body Shop Sunscreens & Lotions (Liquid) The Body Shop/Mark Transfer Co.	Biodegradable Vegetable oil base Unscented/scented Dye-free	47
Earth Science Tanning Lotions (Liquid) Earth Science, Inc.	Biodegradable Vegetable oil base	126
Great Stuff Sunburn Relief (Liquid) 4-D Hobe, Inc.	100% Natural Biodegradable Vegetable oil base	120
Jason Sunbrellas Sunblock (Liquid) Jason Natural Products	Biodegradable Vegetable oil base	11

Product/Manufacturer	Description	Catalog
Jojoba-Aloe Sun Tanning Oil (Liquid) Desert Essence	Biodegradable Vegetable oil base	7, 21
Lily of the Desert Aloe SPF40 (Liquid) Lily of the Desert	Organic aloe vera Biodegradable Vegetable oil base	7
Nature Tan SPF 4 & 8 (Liquid) Aubrey Organics	100% Natural Biodegradable Vegetable oil base	3, 7, 9 45
Orjene Tanning Lotions (Liquid) Orjene Natural Cosmetics	Biodegradable Vegetable oil base	5, 6
Rainbow Sunscreen Lotion (Liquid) Rainbow Research Corp.	Biodegradable Vegetable oil base	4, 116
Real Aloe Suntan Lotion (Liquid) The Real Aloe Co.	Biodegradable Vegetable oil base	7, 115
Sun Milk Tanning Lotion (Liquid) Borlind's of Germany	Biodegradable Vegetable oil base	76
Sunshade 15 Sunblock (Liquid) Aubrey Organics	100% Natural Biodegradable Vegetable oil base	3, 7, 9 45
Tanning Lotions (Liquid) Under the Apple Tree	100% Natural Biodegradable Vegetable oil base	19
The Body Shop Sunscreens (Liquid) The Body Shop, Inc.	Biodegradable Vegetable oil base	127
Wysong Sun Screens & Lotions (Liquid) Wysong Corp.	Biodegradable Vegetable oil base	7

The Bath-room

Product/Manufacturer	Description	Catalog

Deodorants

Product/Manufacturer	Description	Catalog
Aubrey Natural Deodorants (Liquid) Aubrey Organics	100% Natural Biodegradable Vegetable oil base Pump spray/CFC-free	3, 7, 9 45
Le Crystal Deodorant Rock (Bar) Le Crystal Naturel	100% Natural Biodegradable	1, 8, 10 51
Nature de France Deodorants (Stick) Nature de France, Inc.	Biodegradable	5, 6, 21
Nature's Gate Roll-On Deodorants (Liquid) Nature's Gate/Levlad, Inc.	Biodegradable Vegetable oil base	21, 45, 104
Orjene Stick Deodorants (Stick) Orjene Natural Cosmetics	Biodegradable Vegetable oil base	5, 6
Paul Penders Deodorant (Liquid) Paul Penders Products	Biodegradable Vegetable oil base	4, 9, 17
Speick Deodorants (Liquid) Walter Rau Company	100% Natural Biodegradable Vegetable oil base Pump spray/CFC-free	14
Tom's Roll-On Anti-Perspirants (Liquid) Tom's of Maine	Biodegradable Vegetable oil base	2 6, 7 9, 21
Tom's Roll-On/Stick Deodorants (Stick) Tom's of Maine	Biodegradable Vegetable oil base	2, 6, 7 9, 21
Weleda Sage Deodorant (Liquid) Weleda	100% Natural Biodegradable Vegetable oil base Pump spray/CFC-free	2, 5, 9 14, 17, 18 19, 20, 21

Product/Manufacturer	Description	Catalog

Shaving Products

Product/Manufacturer	Description	Catalog
Alba After Shave Balm & Splash (Liquid) Alba Botanica Cosmetics	Biodegradable Vegetable oil base	9, 17, 112
Alba Botanica Cream Shave (Cream) Alba Botanica Cosmetics	Biodegradable Vegetable oil base	9, 17, 112
Azulene Shave Creme (Cream) Earth Science, Inc.	Biodegradable Vegetable oil base	126
Body Shop Aftershave Lotion (Liquid) The Body Shop/Mark Transfer Co.	Biodegradable Vegetable oil base Unscented/scented Dye-free	47
Body Shop Shaving Soap & Gel (Bar) The Body Shop/Mark Transfer Co.	Biodegradable Vegetable oil base Unscented/scented Dye-free	47
Earth Science After Shaves (Liquid) Earth Science, Inc.	Biodegradable Vegetable oil base Pump spray/CFC-free	126
Ginseng Mint Aftershave (Liquid) Aubrey Organics	100% Natural Biodegradable Vegetable oil base	3, 7, 9 45
Mint & Ginseng Shaving Cream (Cream) Aubrey Organics	100% Natural Biodegradable Vegetable oil base	3, 7, 9 45
Mostly Men Aftershave (Liquid) The Body Shop, Inc.	Biodegradable Vegetable oil base	127
Mostly Men Shaving Cream (Liquid) The Body Shop, Inc.	Biodegradable Vegetable oil base	127
Penders After Shave Lotion (Liquid) Paul Penders Products	Biodegradable Vegetable oil base	4, 9, 17
Simmons Aloe Vera Shaving Soap (Bar) Simmons Handcrafts	100% Natural Biodegradable Vegetable oil base	113

The Bath-room

Product/Manufacturer	Description	Catalog
Speick After Shave Gel (Liquid) Walter Rau Company	100% Natural Biodegradable Vegetable oil base	14
Speick Pre Shave Lotion (Liquid) Walter Rau Company	100% Natural Biodegradable Vegetable oil base	14
Tom's Shaving Creams (Cream) Tom's of Maine	100% Natural Biodegradable Vegetable oil base Recycled paper Recyclable aluminum tube	2 6, 7 9, 21
Wysong Shaving Gel (Liquid) Wysong Corp.	100% Natural Biodegradable Vegetable oil base	7

Feminine Hygiene and Cosmetics

Product/Manufacturer	Description	Catalog
Alexandra Avery Perfumes (Liquid) Alexandra Avery	100% Natural Biodegradable	9, 111
Ascent Spray Colognes (Liquid) Santa Fe Fragrance Co.	100% Natural Biodegradable Vegetable oil base	9
Aubrey Eau de Colognes (Liquid) Aubrey Organics	100% Natural Biodegradable Vegetable oil base	3, 7, 9 45
Bare Escentuals Eyeshadows (Powder) Bare Escentuals, Inc.	100% Natural Biodegradable	1, 18, 41
Bare Escentuals Lip Glosses (Cream) Bare Escentuals, Inc.	100% Natural Biodegradable Vegetable oil base	1, 18, 41
Bare Escentuals Lip/Eye Pencils (Sticks) Bare Escentuals, Inc.	100% Natural Biodegradable	1, 18, 41
Bare Escentuals Powders (Powder) Bare Escentuals, Inc.	100% Natural Biodegradable	1, 18, 41

Product/Manufacturer	Description	Catalog
Bee Kind Natural Douche (Liquid) Bee Kind Products	100% Natural Biodegradable Unscented Dye-free	18, 51
Bio-Botanica Herbal Douche (Liquid) Bio-Botanica, Inc.	100% Natural Biodegradable Dye-free Concentrated	19
Borlind's Eye Liner (Stick) Borlind's of Germany	Biodegradable Vegetable oil base	76
Borlind's Eye Shadows (Cream) Borlind's of Germany	Biodegradable Vegetable oil base	76
Borlind's Lip Colors (Stick) Borlind's of Germany	Biodegradable Vegetable oil base	76
Borlind's Make-Up Bases (Cream) Borlind's of Germany	Biodegradable Vegetable oil base	76
Borlind's Mascara (Cream) Borlind's of Germany	Biodegradable	76
Borlind's Powder Rouges (Powder) Borlind's of Germany	Biodegradable Vegetable oil base	76
Colourings Cream Blush (Cream) The Body Shop, Inc.	Biodegradable Vegetable oil base	127
Colourings Eyeshadows (Powder) The Body Shop, Inc.	Biodegradable Vegetable oil base	127
Colourings Lipsticks (Cream) The Body Shop, Inc.	Biodegradable Vegetable oil base	127
Colourings Mascara (Liquid) The Body Shop, Inc.	Biodegradable Vegetable oil base	127

The Bath-room

Product/Manufacturer	Description	Catalog
Colourings Powders (Cream) The Body Shop, Inc.	Biodegradable Vegetable oil base	127
Cycles Mentrual Pads (Cotton) Sisterly Works	100% Natural fibers Biodegradable Unscented Recyclable/reusable	123
Dr. Hauschka Eye Shadows (Cream) Dr. Hauschka Cosmetics, Inc.	100% Natural Biodegradable	1, 9, 14
Dr. Hauschka Lip/Cheek Shades (Cream) Dr. Hauschka Cosmetics, Inc.	100% Natural Biodegradable	1, 9, 14
Eye Make-Up Remover Pads (Cotton) Margarite	100% Natural Biodegradable Vegetable oil base	7
Hygenia Natural Douche (Powder) Women's Health Institute	100% Natural Biodegradable Dye-free	51
Ida Grae Earth Eye/Lip Creme (Cream) Nature's Colors, Ltd.	100% Natural Biodegradable Vegetable oil base	1, 4, 9 41, 45, 102
Ida Grae Earth Eyes Shades (Powder) Nature's Colors, Ltd.	100% Natural Biodegradable Vegetable oil base	1, 4, 9 41, 45, 102
Ida Grae Earth Fragrances (Cream) Nature's Colors, Ltd.	100% Natural Biodegradable Vegetable oil base	1, 4, 9 41, 45, 102
Ida Grae Earth Venus Moisturizer (Liquid) Nature's Colors, Ltd.	100% Natural Biodegradable Vegetable oil base	1, 4, 9 41, 45, 102
Ida Grae Rouges (Powder) Nature's Colors, Ltd.	100% Natural Biodegradable	1, 4, 9 41, 45, 102
Ida Grae Translucent Powder (Powder) Nature's Colors, Ltd.	100% Natural Biodegradable	1, 4, 9 41, 45, 102

Product/Manufacturer	Description	Catalog
Monoi Eau de Toilette (Liquid) Monoi, Inc.	100% Natural Biodegradable Vegetable oil base	9
Natural Cosmetic Brushes (Natural Bristle) Aubrey Organics	100% Natural bristles	3, 7, 9 45
Natural Cosmetic Sponge (Sponge) Aubrey Organics	100% Natural Biodegradable	3, 7, 9 45
Natural Lips Lipsticks (Stick) Aubrey Organics	100% Natural Biodegradable Vegetable oil base	3, 7, 9 45
New Cycle Menstrual Pads (Cotton) Menstrual Health Foundation	100% Natural fiber Biodegradable Recyclable/reusable Unscented	122
Orjene Elastin Foundation (Liquid) Orjene Natural Cosmetics	Biodegradable Water base Unscented	5, 6
Panty Liners (Paper) Seventh Generation	Dioxin-free paper 99% Biodegradable Unscented Packaged in recycled paper	81
Paul Penders Creme Make-Up (Cream) Paul Penders Products	100% Natural Biodegradable	9, 17, 45 104, 105
Paul Penders Eye Pencils (Stick) Paul Penders Products	Biodegradable	9, 17, 45 104, 105
Paul Penders Lipsticks (Stick) Paul Penders Products	100% Natural Biodegradable	9, 17, 45 104, 105
Paul Penders Mascara (Stick) Paul Penders Products	Biodegradable	9, 17, 45 104, 105
Real Aloe Vera Lip Gloss (Liquid) The Real Aloe Co.	Biodegradable Vegetable oil base	7, 115

The Bath-room

Product/Manufacturer	Description	Catalog
Real Purity Creme Foundation (Cream) Real Purity Cosmetics	100% Natural Biodegradable	45
Real Purity Lipsticks (Stick) Real Purity Cosmetics	100% Natural Biodegradable	45
Real Purity Mascara (Liquid) Real Purity Cosmetics	100% Natural Biodegradable	45
Regular Maxi Pads (Paper) Seventh Generation	Dioxin-free paper 99% Biodegradable Unscented Packaged in recycled paper	81
Silken Earth Blush Powders (Powder) Aubrey Organics	100% Natural Biodegradable Vegetable oil base	3, 7, 9 45
Sombra Blushes (Cream) Sombra Cosmetics, Inc.	Biodegradable Vegetable oil base	7, 41, 119
Sombra Foundation Make-Up (Cream) Sombra Cosmetics, Inc.	Biodegradable Vegetable oil base	7, 41, 119
Thin Maxi Pads (Paper) Seventh Generation	Dioxin-free paper 99% Biodegradable Unscented Packaged in recycled paper	81
Unbleached Silk Sea Sponges (Sponge) Sisterly Works	100% Natural Biodegradable Unbleached Unscented Reusable	123
Warm Earth Blushes (Powder) Warm Earth Cosmetics	100% Natural Biodegradable	103, 104
Warm Earth Eye Shadows (Powder) Warm Earth Cosmetics	100% Natural Biodegradable	103, 104
Yeast-Guard (Powder) Women's Health Institute	100% Natural Biodegradable Dye-free	7

CHAPTER 13

The Broom Closet

☞ Mail-Order Product Criteria

The most environmentally desirable products have the following characteristics:

All Cleaning Agents
100 percent natural (no synthetic chemicals), natural fibers (sponges), biodegradable, phosphate-free, chlorine-free; vegetable oil base, unscented, dye-free, concentrated.

Note: All products in this section are chlorine-free.

Product/Manufacturer	Description	Catalog

General-Purpose Cleaners

Product/Manufacturer	Description	Catalog
AFM Safety Clean (Liquid) AFM Enterprises	Phosphate-free No petrochemicals/hydrocarbons	26, 31, 32 33, 34
AFM Super Clean (Liquid) AFM Enterprises	Phosphate-free No petrochemicals/hydrocarbons	26, 31, 32 33, 34
Allen's All-Purpose Cleaner (Liquid) Allen's Naturally	Biodegradable Phosphate-free Unscented Dye-free Concentrated	4, 8, 10 32, 79
Allen's Glass Cleaner (Liquid) Allen's Naturally	Biodegradable Phosphate-free Unscented Dye-free	4, 8, 10 32, 79
Allen's Spray Cleaner (Liquid) Allen's Naturally	Biodegradable Phosphate-free Unscented Dye-free	4, 8, 10 32, 79
Auro Cleansing Emulsion (Liquid) Auro Natural Plant Chemistry	100% Natural Biodegradable Phosphate-free Concentrated	25
Auro Leather Care Cream (Liquid) Auro Natural Plant Chemistry	100% Natural Biodegradable Phosphate-free Concentrated	25
Auro Plant Soap (Liquid) Auro Natural Plant Chemistry	100% Natural Biodegradable Phosphate-free Concentrated	25
Auro Wax-Balm Cleaner (Liquid) Auro Natural Plant Chemistry	100% Natural Biodegradable Phosphate-free Concentrated	25
Avi Soap Concentrate (Liquid) Livos PlantChemistry	100% Natural Biodegradable Phosphate-free Highly concentrated	24, 45, 46

Product/Manufacturer	Description	Catalog
Bertos Leather Seal (Paste) Livos PlantChemistry	100% Natural No petrochemicals/hydrocarbons	24, 45, 46
Ecco Bella Orange Cleaner (Liquid) Ecco Bella	100% Natural Biodegradable Phosphate-free Vegetable oil base	7
Ecover Cream Cleaner (Liquid) Mercantile Food Co.	100% Natural Biodegradable Phosphate-free Vegetable oil base	7, 45, 81 118
Ecover Floor Soap (Liquid) Mercantile Food Co.	100% Natural Biodegradable Phosphate-free Vegetable oil base	7, 45, 81 118
Ecover Heavy Duty Hand Cleaner (Liquid) Mercantile Food Co.	100% Natural Biodegradable Phosphate-free Vegetable oil base	7, 45, 81 118
Ecover Toilet Cleaner (Liquid) Mercantile Food Co.	Biodegradable Phosphate-free Vegetable oil base	7, 45, 81, 118
Glass Cleaner (Liquid) Seventh Generation	Biodegradable Unscented Dye-free Concentrated Recyclable container	81
Granny's Soil Away (Liquid) Granny's Old Fashioned	Phosphate-free Unscented Dye-free	1, 32, 77
Green Cleaner (Liquid) Neo Life	Phosphate-free	8, 38
Homesteaders Hand Soap (Cream) Homesteader & Arnold Co.	100% Natural Biodegradable Phosphate-free Vegetable oil base Dye-free	9

The Broom Closet

Product/Manufacturer	Description	Catalog
Kleen All-Purpose Cleaner (Liquid) Mountain Fresh Products	Biodegradable Phosphate-free Dye-free Concentrated	4, 32, 104 117
Latis Natural Soap (Liquid) Livos PlantChemistry	100% Natural Biodegradable Phosphate-free Vegetable oil base	24, 45, 46
Life Tree Home Soap (Liquid) Sierra Dawn	Biodegradable Phosphate-free	7, 17
Lightening Sweet 'n Clean (Liquid) Lightening Products	100% Natural Biodegradable Vegetable oil base	45
Liquid Enzyme Drain Cleaner (Liquid) Ecco Bella	Biodegradable Phosphate-free	3, 7
New Age Household Cleaner (Liquid) New Age Products	Biodegradable Phosphate-free	4
Rugged Red Cleaner (Liquid) Neo Life	Phosphate-free	8, 38
Snado Leather & Shoe Polish (Paste) Livos PlantChemistry	100% Natural No petrochemicals/hydrocarbons	24, 45, 46

Floor and Furniture Polishes

AFM Polish & Wax (Paste or Liquid) AFM Enterprises	No petrochemicals/hydrocarbons	26, 31-44
Alis Furniture Polish (Liquid) Livos PlantChemistry	100% Natural No petrochemicals/hydrocarbons	24, 45, 46
Auro Arve Plant Polish (Liquid) Auro Natural Plant Chemistry	100% Natural Vegetable oil base Concentrated	25

Product/Manufacturer	Description	Catalog
Auro Beeswax Care (Liquid) Auro Natural Plant Chemistry	100% Natural Concentrated	25
Cembra Pine Furniture Polish (Liquid) Auro Natural Plant Chemistry	100% Natural No petrochemicals/hydrocarbons	25
Dryad Funiture Polish (Liquid) Livos PlantChemistry	100% Natural No petrochemicals/hydrocarbons	24, 45, 46
Gleivo Furniture Wax (Liquid) Livos PlantChemistry	100% Natural No petrochemicals/hydrocarbons	24, 45, 46
Granny's Karpet Kleen (Liquid) Granny's Old Fashioned	Phosphate-free Unscented Dye-free	1, 32, 77
Tekno Cleaner (Liquid) Livos PlantChemistry	100% Natural No petrochemicals/hydrocarbons	24, 45, 46

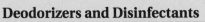

Deodorizers and Disinfectants

Product/Manufacturer	Description	Catalog
AFM X158 Mildew Control (Liquid) AFM Enterprises	Biodegradable No petrochemicals/hydrocarbons	26, 31-44
Air Therapy Disinfectant Fresh (Liquid) Mia Rose Products, Inc.	100% Natural Biodegradable Pump spray/CFC-free	4, 7, 81
Carpet Stuff Deodorizer (Powder) Vermont Herbs	100% Natural Biodegradable	81
Ecco Bella Carpet Freshener (Powder) Ecco Bella	100% Natural Biodegradable	7
Wysong Citressence Deodorizer (Liquid) Wysong Corp.	100% Natural Biodegradable Vegetable oil base	7

CHAPTER 14

The Workshop

☞ Mail-Order Product Criteria

The most environmentally desirable products have the following characteristics:

Paint Products
100 percent natural (no synthetic chemicals), formaldehyde-free, no petrochemicals, no hydrocarbons, water base. Wood preservatives: no creosote, arsenicals. Strippers: no methyl chloride.

Adhesives
100 percent natural (no synthetic chemicals), formaldehyde-free, no petrochemicals, no hydrocarbons, water base.

Product/Manufacturer	Description	Catalog ○

Paint Products

Product/Manufacturer	Description	Catalog
Aidu Radiator Paint (Liquid) Livos PlantChemistry	Natural ingredients Formaldehyde-free	24, 45, 46
Albion White Wash Paint (Liquid) Livos PlantChemistry	Natural ingredients Formaldehyde-free Water base	24, 45, 46
Amellos Enamel Paint (Liquid) Livos PlantChemistry	Natural ingredients Formaldehyde-free	24, 45, 46
Auro Beeswax Floor Finish (Liquid) Auro Natural Plant Chemistry	100% Natural Formaldehyde-free No petrochemicals/hydrocarbons	25
Auro Beeswax Interior Finish (Liquid) Auro Natural Plant Chemistry	100% Natural Formaldehyde-free No petrochemicals/hydrocarbons	25
Auro Borax Wood Preservative (Liquid) Auro Natural Plant Chemistry	100% Natural Formaldehyde-free No petrochemicals/hydrocarbons	25
Auro Clear Oil Primer (Liquid) Auro Natural Plant Chemistry	100% Natural Formaldehyde-free No petrochemicals/hydrocarbons	25
Auro Enamel Primer (Liquid) Auro Natural Plant Chemistry	100% Natural Formaldehyde-free No petrochemicals/hydrocarbons	25
Auro Exterior Wood Stain (Liquid) Auro Natural Plant Chemistry	100% Natural Formaldehyde-free No petrochemicals/hydrocarbons	25
Auro Interior Paint (Liquid) Auro Natural Plant Chemistry	100% Natural Formaldehyde-free No petrochemicals/hydrocarbons Water base	25

Product/Manufacturer	Description	Catalog
Auro Metal Primer (Liquid) Auro Natural Plant Chemistry	100% Natural Formaldehyde-free No petrochemicals/hydrocarbons	25
Auro Resin-Oil Enamel Paint (Liquid) Auro Natural Plant Chemistry	100% Natural Formaldehyde-free No petrochemicals/hydrocarbons	25
Auro Shellac Varnish (Liquid) Auro Natural Plant Chemistry	100% Natural Formaldehyde-free No petrochemicals/hydrocarbons	25
Auro Wood Pitch Preservative (Liquid) Auro Natural Plant Chemistry	100% Natural Formaldehyde-free No petrochemicals/hydrocarbons	25
Bekos Bee & Resin Ointment (Paste) Livos PlantChemistry	Natural ingredients Formaldehyde-free	24, 45, 46
Bela Wood Stain (Liquid) Livos PlantChemistry	100 % Natural Formaldehyde-free No petrochemicals/hydrocarbons Water base	24, 45, 46
Bilo Floor Wax Finish (Paste) Livos PlantChemistry	Natural ingredients Formaldehyde-free	24, 45, 46
Canto Satin Enamel Paint (Liquid) Livos PlantChemistry	Natural ingredients Formaldehyde-free	24, 45, 46
Cem Bond Masonry Paint (Liquid) AFM Enterprises	Formaldehyde-free No petrochemicals/hydrocarbons Water base	26, 31-44
Crystal Aire Clear Finish (Liquid) Pace Chem Industries	Formaldehyde-free No petrochemicals/hydrocarbons Water base	1, 27, 45
Crystal Shield Latex Paint (Liquid) Pace Chem Industries	Formaldehyde-free No petrochemicals/hydrocarbons Water base	27, 45

The Work-Shop

Product/Manufacturer	Description	Catalog
Donnos Wood Pitch Impregnation (Liquid) Livos PlantChemistry	Natural ingredients Formaldehyde-free No creosote No arsenicals	24, 45, 46
Dubno Primer Oil (Liquid) Livos PlantChemistry	Natural ingredients Formaldehyde-free	24, 45, 46
Dubron Wall Paint (Liquid) Livos PlantChemistry	Natural ingredients Formaldehyde-free Water base	24, 45, 46
Duro Metal Primer (Liquid) Livos PlantChemistry	Natural ingredients Formaldehyde-free	24, 45, 46
Dyno Penetrating Water Seal (Liquid) AFM Enterprises	Formaldehyde-free No petrochemicals/hydrocarbons Water base	26, 31-44
Dyno Seal Outdoor Sealer (Liquid) AFM Enterprises	Formaldehyde-free No petrochemicals/hydrocarbons Water base	26, 31-44
Hard Seal Clear Sealant (Liquid) AFM Enterprises	Formaldehyde-free No petrochemicals/hydrocarbons Water base	26, 31-44
Kaldet-Resin & Oil Finish (Liquid) Livos PlantChemistry	Natural ingredients Formaldehyde-free	24, 45, 46
Landis Furniture Shellac (Liquid) Livos PlantChemistry	Natural ingredients Formaldehyde-free	24, 45, 46
Laro-Larch Resin Ointment (Paste) Livos PlantChemistry	Natural ingredients Formaldehyde-free	24, 45, 46
Linus Linseed Impreganation (Liquid) Livos PlantChemistry	Natural ingredients Formaldehyde-free	24, 45, 46
Meldos Hard Sealer (Liquid) Livos PlantChemistry	Natural ingredients Formaldehyde-free	24, 45, 46

Product/Manufacturer	Description	Catalog
Menos Primer (Liquid) Livos PlantChemistry	Natural ingredients Formaldehyde-free	24, 45, 46
Murco Great Latex Flat Paint (Liquid) Murco Wall Products, Inc.	Formaldehyde-free Water base	29
Murco Latex High Gloss Enamel (Liquid) Murco Wall Products, Inc.	Formaldehyde-free Water base	29
Natural Resin Wall Paint (Liquid) Livos PlantChemistry	Natural ingredients Formaldehyde-free Water base	24, 45, 46
Old Fashioned Milk Paint (Powder) Old Fashioned Milk Paint Co.	Formaldehyde-free No petrochemicals/hydrocarbons Water base	28
One Step Seal & Shine (Liquid) AFM Enterprises	Formaldehyde-free No petrochemicals/hydrocarbons	26, 31-44
Polyuraseal Clear Sealer (Liquid) AFM Enterprises	Formaldehyde-free No petrochemicals/hydrocarbons Water base	26, 31-44
Right On Wood Sealing Oil (Liquid) Pace Chem Industries	Formaldehyde-free No petrochemicals/hydrocarbons	27
Safecoat All Purpose Enamel (Liquid) AFM Enterprises	Formaldehyde-free No petrochemicals/hydrocarbons	26, 31-44
Safecoat Paint (Liquid) AFM Enterprises	Formaldehyde-free No petrochemicals/hydrocarbons Water base	26, 31-44
Safecoat Primer Undercoat (Liquid) AFM Enterprises	Formaldehyde-free No petrochemicals/hydrocarbons Water base	26, 31-44
Safecoat Semi Gloss Enamel (Liquid) AFM Enterprises	Formaldehyde-free No petrochemicals/hydrocarbons	26, 31-44

The Work-Shop

Product/Manufacturer	Description	Catalog
Safecoat Wood Stain (Liquid) AFM Enterprises	Formaldehyde-free No petrochemicals/hydrocarbons Water base	26, 31-44
Shingle Protek Sealant (Liquid) AFM Enterprises	Formaldehyde-free No petrochemicals/hydrocarbons	26, 31-44
Taya Wood Glaze (Liquid) Livos PlantChemistry	Natural ingredients Formaldehyde-free	24, 45, 46
Trebo All Purpose Shellac (Liquid) Livos PlantChemistry	Natural ingredients Formaldehyde-free	24, 45, 46
Tunna Furniture Varnish (Liquid) Livos PlantChemistry	Natural ingredients Formaldehyde-free	24, 45, 46
Vindo Enamel Paint (Liquid) Livos PlantChemistry	Natural ingredients Formaldehyde-free	24, 45, 46
Vinyl Block Sealant (Liquid) AFM Enterprises	Formaldehyde-free No petrochemicals/hydrocarbons Water base	26, 31-44
Water Seal Clear Sealant (Liquid) AFM Enterprises	Formaldehyde-free No petrochemicals/hydrocarbons Water base	26, 31-44

Adhesives

Product/Manufacturer	Description	Catalog
3 in 1 Tile Adhesive (Liquid) AFM Enterprises	Formaldehyde-free No petrochemicals/hydrocarbons Water base	26, 31-44
AFM Carpet Adhesive (Liquid) AFM Enterprises	Formaldehyde-free No petrochemicals/hydrocarbons	26, 31-44
AFM Wallpaper Adhesive (Liquid) AFM Enterprises	Formaldehyde-free No petrochemicals/hydrocarbons Water base	26, 31-44

Product/Manufacturer	Description	Catalog
Auro Carpet Adhesive (Liquid) Auro Natural Plant Chemistry	100% Natural Formaldehyde-free No petrochemicals/hydrocarbons Water base	25
Auro Cork Adhesive (Liquid) Auro Natural Plant Chemistry	100% Natural Formaldehyde-free No petrochemicals/hydrocarbons Water base	25
Auro Linoleum Adhesive (Liquid) Auro Natural Plant Chemistry	100% Natural Formaldehyde-free No petrochemicals/hydrocarbons Water base	25
Auro Parquet Adhesive (Liquid) Auro Natural Plant Chemistry	100% Natural Formaldehyde-free No petrochemicals/hydrocarbons Water base	25
Auro Tile Adhesive (Liquid) Auro Natural Plant Chemistry	100% Natural Formaldehyde-free No petrochemicals/hydrocarbons Water base	25
Auro Wall Paper Adhesive (Liquid) Auro Natural Plant Chemistry	100% Natural Formaldehyde-free No petrochemicals/hydrocarbons Water base	25
Auro Wood Adhesive (Liquid) Auro Natural Plant Chemistry	100% Natural Formaldehyde-free No petrochemicals/hydrocarbons Water base	25
Lavo Wallpaper Paste (Paste) Livos PlantChemistry	100% Natural Formaldehyde-free No petrochemicals/hydrocarbons Water base	24, 45, 46
Linami Cork Adhesive (Liquid) Livos PlantChemistry	Natural ingredients Formaldehyde-free Water base	24, 45, 46

The Work-Shop

Product/Manufacturer	Description	Catalog

Miscellaneous Building Products

Product/Manufacturer	Description	Catalog
AFM Joint Compound (Paste) AFM Enterprises	Formaldehyde-free No petrochemicals/hydrocarbons Water base	26, 31-44
AFM Spackling Compound (Paste) AFM Enterprises	Formaldehyde-free No petrochemicals/hydrocarbons Water base	26, 31-44
AFM Tile Grout (Paste) AFM Enterprises	Formaldehyde-free No petrochemicals/hydrocarbons Water base	26, 31-44
AFM Tile Grout Release (Paste) AFM Enterprises	Formaldehyde-free No petrochemicals/hydrocarbons Water base	26, 31-44
Anavo Oil-Based Spackel (Paste) Livos PlantChemistry	Natural ingredients Formaldehyde-free	24, 45, 46
Auro Alcohol Thinner (Liquid) Auro Natural Plant Chemistry	100% Natural Formaldehyde-free No petrochemicals/hydrocarbons	25
Auro Citrus Oil Thinner (Liquid) Auro Natural Plant Chemistry	100% Natural Formaldehyde-free No petrochemicals/hydrocarbons	25
Auro Joint Filler (Liquid) Auro Natural Plant Chemistry	100% Natural Formaldehyde-free No petrochemicals/hydrocarbons Water base	25
Auro Paint Remover (Paste) Auro Natural Plant Chemistry	100% Natural Formaldehyde-free No petrochemicals/hydrocarbons	25
Auro Tile Grout (Liquid) Auro Natural Plant Chemistry	100% Natural Formaldehyde-free No petrochemicals/hydrocarbons Water base	25
Dyno Flex Caulking Compound (Paste) AFM Enterprises	Formaldehyde-free No petrochemicals/hydrocarbons Water base	26, 31-44

Product/Manufacturer	Description	Catalog
Dyno Flex Mastic Sealer (Paste) AFM Enterprises	Formaldehyde-free No petrochemicals/hydrocarbons Water base	26, 31-44
Kiros Alcohol Thinner (Liquid) Livos PlantChemistry	Natural ingredients Formaldehyde-free	24, 45, 46
Leinos Citrus Thinner (Liquid) Livos PlantChemistry	Natural ingredients Formaldehyde-free	24, 45, 46
Linseed Putty (Paste) Livos PlantChemistry	Natural ingredients Formaldehyde-free	24, 45, 46
Murco Joint Compound (Powder) Murco Wall Products, Inc.	Formaldehyde-free Water base	29
Stripper 66 (Liquid) AFM Enterprises	Formaldehyde-free No petrochemicals/hydrocarbons No methylene chloride	26, 31-44
Vedo Spackling Compound (Powder) Livos PlantChemistry	Natural ingredients Formaldehyde-free	24, 45, 46

The Work-Shop

CHAPTER 15

The Yard and Pet Supplies

☞ Mail-Order Product Criteria

The most environmentally desirable products have the following characteristics:

Yard

Pest Control Products and Fertilizers
100 percent natural (no synthetic chemicals), biodegradable; no organo-phosphates, no arsenicals, no chlorinated hydrocarbons, concentrated.

Lawn Bags
Paper only.

Pet Supplies

Flea and Tick Products
100 percent natural (no synthetic chemicals), biodegradable; no organo-phosphates, no arsenicals, no chlorinated hydrocarbons, reusable packaging.

Regular Pet Shampoos
100 percent natural (no synthetic chemicals), biodegradable, vegetable oil base.

Cat Litter
Dust-free, no perfumes.

Product/Manufacturer	Description	Catalog

Pest-Control Products

Product/Manufacturer	Description	Catalog
African Violet Insect Killer (Liquid) Safer	100% Natural Biodegradable No organo-phosphates No arsenicals No chlorinated hydrocarbons	84, 85, 86
Ant-Free (Liquid) Snoek	100% Natural Biodegradable No organo-phosphates No arsenicals . No chlorinated hydrocarbons	86
Aphid, Whitefly Killer (Liquid) Safer	100% Natural Biodegradable No organo-phosphates No arsenicals No chlorinated hydrocarbons	84, 85, 86
Aphid-Mite Attack (Liquid) Ringer	100% Natural Biodegradable No organo-phosphates No arsenicals No chlorinated hydrocarbons	84, 86, 88
B.t. Caterpillar Killer (Liquid) Safer	100% Natural Biodegradable No organo-phosphates No arsenicals No chlorinated hydrocarbons Concentrated	84, 85, 86
Biolure Pest Traps (Paper/Plastic) Biolure	No organo-phosphates No arsenicals No chlorinated hydrocarbons	99
Clandosan Nematode Control (Granular) Safer	100% Natural Biodegradable No organo-phosphates No arsenicals No chlorinated hydrocarbons	84, 85, 86
Colorado Potato Beetle Beater (Liquid) Bonide	Biodegradable No organo-phosphates No arsenicals No chlorinated hydrocarbons	90

Product/Manufacturer	Description	Catalog
Crawling Insect Attack (Liquid) Ringer	100% Natural Biodegradable No organo-phosphates No arsenicals No chlorinated hydrocarbons	84, 86, 88
Diatom Dust (Powder) Necessary Trading Co.	100% Natural Biodegradable No organo-phosphates No arsenicals No chlorinated hydrocarbons	85, 86, 88 99
Dipel Dust (Powder) Bonide	Biodegradable No organo-phosphates No arsenicals No chlorinated hydrocarbons	85, 88, 90
Dis-Patch (Powder/Granular) Ringer	100% Natural Biodegradable No organo-phosphates No arsenicals No chlorinated hydrocarbons	84, 86, 88
ENTIRE Flea & Tick Spray (Liquid) Safer	100% Natural Biodegradable No organo-phosphates No arsenicals No chlorinated hydrocarbons	84, 85, 86
ENTIRE Insect Killer for Trees (Liquid) Safer	100% Natural Biodegradable No organo-phosphates No arsenicals No chlorinated hydrocarbons	84, 85, 86
ENTIRE Insect Killer for Yards (Liquid) Safer	100% Natural Biodegradable No organo-phosphates No arsenicals No chlorinated hydrocarbons	84, 85, 86
Early Alert Trapstix (Paper) Safer	100% Natural Biodegradable No organo-phosphates No arsenicals No chlorinated hydrocarbons	84, 85, 86
EcoSafe Pyrethrum Insect Powder (Powder) EcoSafe Laboratories	Biodegradable No organo-phosphates No arsenicals No chlorinated hydrocarbons	88

Yard
and
Pet

Product/Manufacturer	Description	Catalog
Flea & Tick Attack (Liquid) Ringer	100% Natural Biodegradable No organo-phosphates No arsenicals No chlorinated hydrocarbons	84, 86, 88
Flying Insect Attack (Bars) Ringer	100% Natural Biodegradable No organo-phosphates No arsenicals No chlorinated hydrocarbons	84, 86, 88
Garden Dust (Powder) Bonide	Biodegradable No organo-phosphates No arsenicals No chlorinated hydrocarbons	85, 90
Garden Fungicide (Liquid) Safer	100% Natural Biodegradable No organo-phosphates No arsenicals No chlorinated hydrocarbons	84, 85, 86
Garden Insect Killer (Liquid) Safer	100% Natural Biodegradable No organo-phosphates No arsenicals No chlorinated hydrocarbons	84, 85, 86
Garden Insecticidal Soap (Liquid) Safer	100% Natural Biodegradable No organo-phosphates No arsenicals No chlorinated hydrocarbons Concentrated	84, 85, 86
Grasshopper Control (Granular) Safer	100% Natural Biodegradable No organo-phosphates No arsenicals No chlorinated hydrocarbons	84, 85, 86
Green Ban for Plants (Powder) Mulgum Hollow Farm	100% Natural Biodegradable No organo-phosphates No arsenicals No chlorinated hydrocarbons	85, 86, 88 99

Product/Manufacturer	Description	Catalog
Grub Attack (Powder/Granular) Ringer	100% Natural Biodegradable No organo-phosphates No arsenicals No chlorinated hydrocarbons	84, 86, 88
Grub Killer (Powder) Safer	100% Natural Biodegradable No organo-phosphates No arsenicals No chlorinated hydrocarbons	84, 85, 86
Hinder Deer & Rabbit Repellant (Liquid) Leffingwell	100% Natural Biodegradable No organo-phosphates No arsenicals No chlorinated hydrocarbons	86, 99
Insect Soap for Fruits & Vegetables (Liquid) Safer	100% Natural Biodegradable No organo-phosphates No arsenicals No chlorinated hydrocarbons	84, 85, 86
Insect Soap for Houseplants (Liquid) Safer	100% Natural Biodegradable No organo-phosphates No arsenicals No chlorinated hydrocarbons Concentrated	84, 85, 86
Insect Soap for Roses & Flower (Liquid) Safer	100% Natural Biodegradable No organo-phosphates No arsenicals No chlorinated hydrocarbons	84, 85, 86
Japanese Beetle Killer (Liquid) Safer	100% Natural Biodegradable No organo-phosphates No arsenicals No chlorinated hydrocarbons	84, 85, 86
Mite Killer (Liquid) Safer	100% Natural Biodegradable No organo-phosphates No arsenicals No chlorinated hydrocarbons	84, 85, 86

Yard and Pet

Product/Manufacturer	Description	Catalog
Moss & Algae Killer for Decks (Liquid) Safer	100% Natural Biodegradable No organo-phosphates No arsenicals No chlorinated hydrocarbons	84, 85, 86
Moss Killer for Lawns (Liquid) Safer	100% Natural Biodegradable No organo-phosphates No arsenicals No chlorinated hydrocarbons Concentrated	84, 85, 86
Pyrenone Crop Spray (Liquid) Bonide	Biodegradable No organo-phosphates No arsenicals No chlorinated hydrocarbons	90
Ro-Pel (Liquid) Burlington Scientific Corp.	100% Natural Biodegradable No organo-phosphates No arsenicals No chlorinated hydrocarbons	84, 86, 88 99
Rotenone (Powder/Liquid) Bonide	Biodegradable No organo-phosphates No arsenicals No chlorinated hydrocarbons	85, 86, 88 90, 99
Rotenone/Pyrethrin Spray (Liquid) Bonide	Biodegradable No organo-phosphates No arsenicals No chlorinated hydrocarbons	85, 90
Sabadilla Red Devil (Powder) Necessary Trading Co.	100% Natural Biodegradable No organo-phosphates No arsenicals No chlorinated hydrocarbons	85, 86, 88 90, 99
Safer Traps-Housefly (Plastic) Safer	100% Natural Biodegradable No organo-phosphates No arsenicals No chlorinated hydrocarbons	84, 85, 86
Safer Traps-Japanese Beetles (Paper) Safer	100% Natural Biodegradable No organo-phosphates No arsenicals No chlorinated hydrocarbons	84, 85, 86

Product/Manufacturer	Description	Catalog
Scanmask (Liquid) Scanmask	100% Natural Biodegradable No organo-phosphates No arsenicals No chlorinated hydrocarbons	84, 86, 88 99
Schnecken Slug Repellent (Pellets) Snoek	100% Natural Biodegradable No organo-phosphates No arsenicals No chlorinated hydrocarbons	86
SharpShooter Weed Killer (Liquid) Safer	100% Natural Biodegradable No organo-phosphates No arsenicals No chlorinated hydrocarbons	84, 85, 86
SilKaBen Plant Protector (Powder) Snoek	100% Natural Biodegradable No organo-phosphates No arsenicals No chlorinated hydrocarbons	86
Tomato Worm Attack (Powder) Ringer	100% Natural Biodegradable No organo-phosphates No arsenicals No chlorinated hydrocarbons	84, 86, 88
Tomato Worm Attack (Powder) Ringer	100% Natural Biodegradable No organo-phosphates No arsenicals No chlorinated hydrocarbons	84, 86, 88
Vegetable Insect Attack (Powder) Ringer	100% Natural Biodegradable No organo-phosphates No arsenicals No chlorinated hydrocarbons	84, 86, 88
Wasp & Hornet Attack (Liquid) Ringer	100% Natural Biodegradable No organo-phosphates No arsenicals No chlorinated hydrocarbons	84, 86, 88

Yard
and
Pet

Product/Manufacturer	Description	Catalog
Yard & Garden Insect Attack (Liquid) Ringer	100% Natural Biodegradable No organo-phosphates No arsenicals No chlorinated hydrocarbons	84, 86, 88
Zap Ant & Roach Powder (Powder) EcoSafe Laboratories	100% Natural Biodegradable No organo-phosphates No arsenicals No chlorinated hydrocarbons	85, 86, 88 99

Fertilizers

Product/Manufacturer	Description	Catalog
All & Only Natural Garden Food (Powder) F & B	100% Natural Biodegradable No organo-phosphates No arsenicals No chlorinated hydrocarbons	86, 99
Bay Crab Meal Fertilizer (Powder) Gardener's Supply	100% Natural Biodegradable No organo-phosphates No arsenicals No chlorinated hydrocarbons	86, 99
Berry Booster (Powder) Ringer	100% Natural Biodegradable No organo-phosphates No arsenicals No chlorinated hydrocarbons	84, 86, 88
BioActivator Compost Activator (Powder) Necessary Trading Co.	100% Natural Biodegradable No organo-phosphates No arsenicals No chlorinated hydrocarbons	85
BioCast Fertilizer (Powder) Necessary Trading Co.	100% Natural Biodegradable No organo-phosphates No arsenicals No chlorinated hydrocarbons	85, 86, 99
BioSafe (Powder) BioSafe Products	100% Natural Biodegradable No organo-phosphates No arsenicals No chlorinated hydrocarbons	85, 86, 90 99

Product/Manufacturer	Description	Catalog
Brown Leaf Compost Maker (Powder) Ringer	100% Natural Biodegradable No organo-phosphates No arsenicals No chlorinated hydrocarbons	84, 86, 88
Compost Life (Powder) Necessary Trading Co.	100% Natural Biodegradable No organo-phosphates No arsenicals No chlorinated hydrocarbons	85
Compost Plus (Powder) Ringer	100% Natural Biodegradable No organo-phosphates No arsenicals No chlorinated hydrocarbons	84, 86, 88
Erth-Rite "C" Fertilizer (Powder) Erth-Rite	100% Natural Biodegradable No organo-phosphates No arsenicals No chlorinated hydrocarbons	45, 99
Erth-Rite Lawn 3-2-2 (Powder) Erth-Rite	100% Natural Biodegradable No organo-phosphates No arsenicals No chlorinated hydrocarbons	45, 99
Fertrell 1 Fish Fertilizer (Liquid) Fertrell Co.	100% Natural Biodegradable No organo-phosphates No arsenicals No chlorinated hydrocarbons	99
Fertrell Super 3-2-3 (Powders) Fertrell Co.	100% Natural Biodegradable No organo-phosphates No arsenicals No chlorinated hydrocarbons	99
Fertrell Super-N 4-2-4 (Powder) Fertrell Co.	100% Natural Biodegradable No organo-phosphates No arsenicals No chlorinated hydrocarbons	99

Yard and Pet

Product/Manufacturer	Description	Catalog
Flower Garden Restore (Powder) Ringer	100% Natural Biodegradable No organo-phosphates No arsenicals No chlorinated hydrocarbons	84, 86, 88
Flowers Alive! Plant Food (Powder) Natural Gardening Research	100% Natural Biodegradable No organo-phosphates No arsenicals No chlorinated hydrocarbons	88
FoliaGro Plant Food (Powder) Necessary Trading Co.	100% Natural Biodegradable No organo-phosphates No arsenicals No chlorinated hydrocarbons	85, 86, 88 99
ForEverGreen Plant Protectant (Liquid) Safer	100% Natural Biodegradable No organo-phosphates No arsenicals No chlorinated hydrocarbons	84, 85, 86
Fruit Tree Booster (Powder) Ringer	100% Natural Biodegradable No organo-phosphates No arsenicals No chlorinated hydrocarbons	84, 86, 88
Gardener's Supply Bat Guano (Powder) Gardener's Supply	100% Natural Biodegradable No organo-phosphates No arsenicals No chlorinated hydrocarbons	86
Gardener's Supply Flower Food (Powder) Gardener's Supply	100% Natural Biodegradable No organo-phosphates No arsenicals No chlorinated hydrocarbons	86
Gotta Grow Energy Buttons (Powder) Gardener's Supply	100% Natural Biodegradable No organo-phosphates No arsenicals No chlorinated hydrocarbons	86

Product/Manufacturer	Description	Catalog
Grass Clippings Compost Maker (Powder) Ringer	100% Natural Biodegradable No organo-phosphates No arsenicals No chlorinated hydrocarbons	84, 86, 88
Grass-Patch Growing System (Powder) Ringer	100% Natural Biodegradable No organo-phosphates No arsenicals No chlorinated hydrocarbons	84, 86, 88
Houseplants Alive! Plant Food (Powder) Natural Gardening Research	100% Natural Biodegradable No organo-phosphates No arsenicals No chlorinated hydrocarbons	88
Lawn Restore (Powder) Ringer	100% Natural Biodegradable No organo-phosphates No arsenicals No chlorinated hydrocarbons	84, 86, 88
Leafclean & Lustre (Liquid) Safer	100% Natural Biodegradable No organo-phosphates No arsenicals No chlorinated hydrocarbons	84, 85, 86
Naturelease for Tomatoes (Powder) Ringer	100% Natural Biodegradable No organo-phosphates No arsenicals No chlorinated hydrocarbons	84, 86, 88
Paygro Composted Cow Manure (Powder) Paygro Inc.	100% Natural Biodegradable No organo-phosphates No arsenicals No chlorinated hydrocarbons	85
Plant Right Plant Food (Pellets) Plant Right Products	100% Natural Biodegradable No organo-phosphates No arsenicals No chlorinated hydrocarbons	99

Yard and Pet

Product/Manufacturer	Description	Catalog
Potato Booster (Powder) Ringer	100% Natural Biodegradable No organo-phosphates No arsenicals No chlorinated hydrocarbons	84, 86, 88
ReStart Starter **Fertilizer (Powder)** Ringer	100% Natural Biodegradable No organo-phosphates No arsenicals No chlorinated hydrocarbons	84, 86, 88
Ready-Made Compost **(Powder)** Ringer	100% Natural Biodegradable No organo-phosphates No arsenicals No chlorinated hydrocarbons	84, 86, 88
Restore for Bulbs **(Powder)** Ringer	100% Natural Biodegradable No organo-phosphates No arsenicals No chlorinated hydrocarbons	84, 86, 88
Restore for Foliage **Plants (Powder)** Ringer	100% Natural Biodegradable No organo-phosphates No arsenicals No chlorinated hydrocarbons	84, 86, 88
Roots Fertilizer **(Liquid)** Roots Organics	100% Natural Biodegradable No organo-phosphates No arsenicals No chlorinated hydrocarbons	85, 86, 99
Roots Plus Fertilizer **(Liquid)** Roots Organics	100% Natural Biodegradable No organo-phosphates No arsenicals No chlorinated hydrocarbons	85, 86, 99
Rose Restore (Powder) Ringer	100% Natural Biodegradable No organo-phosphates No arsenicals No chlorinated hydrocarbons	84, 86, 88

Product/Manufacturer	Description	Catalog
Sea Crop Seaweed Fertilizer (Liquid) Sea Crop	100% Natural Biodegradable No organo-phosphates No arsenicals No chlorinated hydrocarbons Concentrated	99
Sea Crop Seaweed Powder (Powder) Sea Crop	100% Natural Biodegradable No organo-phosphates No arsenicals No chlorinated hydrocarbons Highly concentrated	99
Sea Mix Fish/Seaweed Fertilizer (Liquid) Sea Crop	100% Natural Biodegradable No organo-phosphates No arsenicals No chlorinated hydrocarbons Concentrated	99
Shrub Restore (Powder) Ringer	100% Natural Biodegradable No organo-phosphates No arsenicals No chlorinated hydrocarbons	84, 86, 88
Soil Vitalize (Powder) Necessary Trading Co.	100% Natural Biodegradable No organo-phosphates No arsenicals No chlorinated hydrocarbons	85
Strawberry Booster (Powder) Ringer	100% Natural Biodegradable No organo-phosphates No arsenicals No chlorinated hydrocarbons	84, 86, 88
Stump Remover (Powder) Ringer	100% Natural Biodegradable No organo-phosphates No arsenicals No chlorinated hydrocarbons	84, 86, 88
Super Plant Food (Powder) Fertrell Co.	100% Natural Biodegradable No organo-phosphates No arsenicals No chlorinated hydrocarbons	86, 99

Yard and Pet

Product/Manufacturer	Description	Catalog
Sustane 5-2-4 Lawn Fertilizer (Granular) Sustane	100% Natural Biodegradable No organo-phosphates No arsenicals No chlorinated hydrocarbons	85, 86, 99
Thorvin Kelp Fertilizer (Powder) Necessary Trading Co.	100% Natural Biodegradable No organo-phosphates No arsenicals No chlorinated hydrocarbons	85, 86, 99
Tomato Restore (Powder) Ringer	100% Natural Biodegradable No organo-phosphates No arsenicals No chlorinated hydrocarbons	84, 86, 88
Vegetable Garden Restore (Powder) Ringer	100% Natural Biodegradable No organo-phosphates No arsenicals No chlorinated hydrocarbons	84, 86, 88
Vegetables Alive! Plant Food (Powder) Natural Gardening Research	100% Natural Biodegradable No organo-phosphates No arsenicals No chlorinated hydrocarbons	88
Winter Garden Soil Restore (Powder) Ringer	100% Natural Biodegradable No organo-phosphates No arsenicals No chlorinated hydrocarbons	84, 86, 88
WinterStore for Lawns (Powder) Ringer	100% Natural Biodegradable No organo-phosphates No arsenicals No chlorinated hydrocarbons	84, 86, 88

Lawn and Leaf Bags

30 Gal. Paper Leaf Bags (Paper) SetPoint, Inc.	Biodegradable Recyclable/reusable	81, 118

Product/Manufacturer	Description	Catalog
Ecolobag Paper Leaf Bags (Paper) Dano Enterprises	Biodegradable Recyclable	100
Hortopaper Biodegradable Mulch Gardener's Supply	100% Biodegradable Recycled paper and peat moss	86

Pet-Care Products

Product/Manufacturer	Description	Catalog
100% Pyrethrum Powder (Powder) EcoSafe Laboratories	100% Natural Biodegradable No organo-phosphates No arsenicals No chlorinated hydrocarbons	88
4-D Bug & Pest Control (Powder) 4-D Hobe, Inc.	100% Natural Biodegradable No organo-phosphates No arsenicals No chlorinated hydrocarbons	120
Aloe Vera Repellent Shampoo (Liquid) Nature's Gate/Levlad, Inc.	Biodegradable Vegetable oil base No organo-phosphates No arsenicals No chlorinated hydrocarbons	2, 15, 105
Attack Conditioning Pet Shampoo (Liquid) Ringer	100% Natural Biodegradable No organo-phosphates No arsenicals No chlorinated hydrocarbons	45, 84
Azulene Bluing Pet Shampoo (Liquid) Nature's Gate/Levlad, Inc.	Biodegradable Vegetable oil base	2, 15, 105
Carpet/House/Kennel Spray (Liquid) Flea Flea Products	100% Natural Biodegradable No organo-phosphates No arsenicals No chlorinated hydrocarbons	107
Cat-Ex Flea Treatment (Liquid) Pet Organics	Biodegradable No organo-phosphates No arsenicals No chlorinated hydrocarbons	38

Yard
and
Pet

Product/Manufacturer	Description	Catalog
Coat Conditioner for Dogs (Liquid) Safer	100% Natural Biodegradable No organo-phosphates No arsenicals No chlorinated hydrocarbons	83, 86, 88 99, 107
Dog-Ex Flea Treatment (Liquid) Pet Organics	Biodegradable No organo-phosphates No arsenicals No chlorinated hydrocarbons	38
ENTIRE Flea & Tick Spray (Liquid) Safer	100% Natural Biodegradable No organo-phosphates No arsenicals No chlorinated hydrocarbons	83, 86, 88 99, 107
Flea & Tick Attack (Liquid) Ringer	100% Natural Biodegradable No organo-phosphates No arsenicals No chlorinated hydrocarbons	45, 84
Flea Be Gone Powder (Powder) Avena Botanicals	100% Natural Biodegradable No organo-phosphates No arsenicals No chlorinated hydrocarbons	109
Flea Be Gone Soap (Liquid) Avena Botanicals	100% Natural Biodegradable No organo-phosphates No arsenicals No chlorinated hydrocarbons	109
Flea Flea Bar Soap (Bar) Flea Flea Products	100% Natural Biodegradable No organo-phosphates No arsenicals No chlorinated hydrocarbons	107
Flea Flea Pet Shampoo (Liquid) Flea Flea Products	100% Natural Biodegradable No organo-phosphates No arsenicals No chlorinated hydrocarbons	107

Product/Manufacturer	Description	Catalog
Flea Flea Pet Spray (Liquid) Flea Flea Products	100% Natural Biodegradable No organo-phosphates No arsenicals No chlorinated hydrocarbons	107
Flea-Relief (Liquid) Dr. Goodpet Products	100% Natural Biodegradable No organo-phosphates No arsenicals No chlorinated hydrocarbons	9, 107
Gentle Dragon Wormer-Cats & Dogs (Powder) EcoSafe Laboratories	100% Natural Biodegradable No organo-phosphates No arsenicals No chlorinated hydrocarbons	7, 32, 105
Golden Lemon Shampoo-Dog/Cat (Liquid) Safer	100% Natural Biodegradable No organo-phosphates No arsenicals No chlorinated hydrocarbons	83, 86, 88 99, 107
Green Ban Dog Shampoo (Liquid) Mulgum Hollow Farm	100% Natural Biodegradable No organo-phosphates No arsenicals No chlorinated hydrocarbons	7, 32, 105
Green Ban Flea Powder (Powder) Mulgum Hollow Farm	100% Natural Biodegradable No organo-phosphates No arsenicals No chlorinated hydrocarbons	7, 9, 32 37, 48, 86 105
Hargate Insect Spray (Liquid) Hargate	Biodegradable No organo-phosphates No arsenicals No chlorinated hydrocarbons	118
Herbal Animal Shampoo Concentrate (Liquid) EcoSafe Laboratories	100% Natural Biodegradable No organo-phosphates No arsenicals No chlorinated hydrocarbons Concentrated	9, 32, 88 105
Herbal Pet Coat Conditioner (Liquid) Nature's Gate/Levlad, Inc.	Biodegradable Vegetable oil base	2, 15, 105

Yard and Pet

Product/Manufacturer	Description	Catalog
Hot Spot Lotion (Liquid) Flea Flea Products	100% Natural Biodegradable No organo-phosphates No arsenicals No chlorinated hydrocarbons	107
Indoor Flea Guard (Liquid) Safer	100% Natural Biodegradable No organo-phosphates No arsenicals No chlorinated hydrocarbons	83, 86, 88 99, 107
Kleen Pet Flea Shampoo (Liquid) Pet Organics	Biodegradable No organo-phosphates No arsenicals No chlorinated hydrocarbons	38
Lightening Cat Shampoo (Liquid) Lightening Products	100% Natural Biodegradable Vegetable oil base	9, 45, 107
Lightening Cat Spray (Liquid) Lightening Products	100% Natural Biodegradable Vegetable oil base	9, 45, 107
Lightening Dog Shampoo (Liquid) Lightening Products	100% Natural Biodegradable Vegetable oil base	9, 45, 107
Lightening Sweet & Clean (Liquid) Lightening Products	100% Natural Biodegradable No organo-phosphates No arsenicals No chlorinated hydrocarbons Vegetable oil base	9, 45, 107
Nature's Gate Pet Shampoo (Liquid) Nature's Gate/Levlad, Inc.	100% Natural Biodegradable Vegetable oil base	2, 15, 105
Organimals Dip & Creme Rinse (Liquid) Aubrey Organics	100% Natural Biodegradable Vegetable oil base	3, 6
Organimals Grooming Spray (Liquid) Aubrey Organics	100% Natural Biodegradable Vegetable oil base	3, 6
Organimals Pet Shampoo (Liquid) Aubrey Organics	100% Natural Biodegradable Vegetable oil base	3, 6

Product/Manufacturer	Description	Catalog
POW Herbal Flea Powder (Powder) EcoSafe Laboratories	100% Natural Biodegradable No organo-phosphates No arsenicals No chlorinated hydrocarbons	32, 45, 88 105
Pet Guard Herbal Flea Collar (Liquid/Fabric) Pet Guard	100% Natural Biodegradable No organo-phosphates No arsenicals No chlorinated hydrocarbons Rechargeable/reusable	6
Rechargeable Herbal Flea Collar (Liquid/Fabric) EcoSafe Laboratories	100% Natural Biodegradable No organo-phosphates No arsenicals No chlorinated hydrocarbons Reusable	7, 9, 45 88, 107
Royal Herbal Flea Collars (Liquid/Leather) Royal Herbal Products	100% Natural Biodegradable No organo-phosphates No arsenicals No chlorinated hydrocarbons Rechargeable/reusable	14, 108
Royal Herbal Pet Powder (Powder) Royal Herbal Products	100% Natural Biodegradable No organo-phosphates No arsenicals No chlorinated hydrocarbons	14, 108
Royal Herbal Pet Shampoo (Liquid) Royal Herbal Products	100% Natural Biodegradable Vegetable oil base No organo-phosphates No arsenicals No chlorinated hydrocarbons	14, 108
Royal Herbal Skin Ointment (Liquid) Royal Herbal Products	100% Natural Biodegradable Vegetable oil base No organo-phosphates No arsenicals No chlorinated hydrocarbons	14, 108

Yard
and
Pet

Product/Manufacturer	Description	Catalog
Safer Pet Odor Eliminator (Liquid) Safer	100% Natural Biodegradable No organo-phosphates No arsenicals No chlorinated hydrocarbons	83, 86, 88 99, 107
Safer's Flea Soap for Dogs/Cats (Liquid) Safer	100% Natural Biodegradable No organo-phosphates No arsenicals No chlorinated hydrocarbons	83, 86, 88 99, 107
Silk Protein Pet Shampoo (Liquid) Nature's Gate/Levlad, Inc.	Biodegradable Vegetable oil base Concentrated	2, 15, 105
Skin & Coat Conditioner (Liquid) Pet Organics	Biodegradable No organo-phosphates No arsenicals No chlorinated hydrocarbons	38
Spritz Dog/Cat Coat Enhancer (Liquid) EcoSafe Laboratories	100% Natural Biodegradable .	9, 86, 88 96
Tea Tree Anti-Itch Pet Shampoo (Liquid) Thursday Plantation Products	Biodegradable No organo-phosphates No arsenicals No chlorinated hydrocarbons	9

CHAPTER 16

The Garage

☞ Mail-Order Product Criteria

The most environmentally desirable products have the following characteristics:

Motor oil
Recycled contents and packaging.

Cleaning products
100 percent natural, biodegradable, phosphate-free, concentrated, recycled and/or recyclable packaging.

Note: At this time, there are very few mail-order green automotive products available, so no product listings have been provided. CAM2 Green Line Motor Oil is recycled and can be bought through the Seventh Generation catalog (#81—see page 234). Apply the same environmental standards to car cleaning products as you would to kitchen, bathroom, and general cleansers listed in "The Mail Order Shopper's Guide."

PART III

A Guide to Environmental Issues

T HIS GUIDE IS designed to give you a quick understanding of the major environmental issues and challenges that we all face. Think of it as an owner's manual for the environment. As you peruse the entries, keep in mind that every action you take as a consumer has an environmental impact that extends to the remote areas of the globe. Likewise, events happening far away may someday affect you very directly. Read on and find out how the pressure in your car's tires can affect the health of rivers and streams in another state. Find out why your next outdoor barbecue might be contributing to an increase in skin cancer in places hundreds or thousands of miles away. And most important, find out why the repair and maintenance of the environment is everyone's business, whether they live in Manhattan or Timbuktu.

Here are the basics that all green consumers should know:

Acid Rain

Normally, rainwater is slightly acidic because of carbon dioxide dissolved in it. This produces very dilute carbonic acid, similar to that found in carbonated beverages. But when sulfur dioxide and nitrogen oxides are released into the atmosphere during the combustion of fuels, they also dissolve in rainwater and produce the much stronger nitric and sulfuric acids. The term "acid rain" refers to rain, snow, fog, and even dry air in which the concentration of acid is from 10 to 1,000 times higher than normal.

Acid rain has a variety of harmful effects on the environment. It weakens many types of trees, making them more susceptible to fungi and other infections. Acid rain is responsible for the loss of millions of acres of forests in Europe alone. And the maple syrup industry in parts of Canada and New England has been severely impaired due to the destruction of sugar maples.

Acidity also kills wildlife in rivers and streams, making it impossible for many fish to reproduce, and decimating the microorganisms that serve as their food sources. In addition, acid water dissolves aluminum, nickel, zinc, lead, and other toxic metals in soil. These metals can kill fish and other aquatic organisms when rainwater washes over the soil and empties into streams and rivers. According to the U.S. Office of Technology Assessment, at least 3,000 lakes and 23,000 miles of streams east of the Mississippi River are extremely vulnerable to acid rain or have already become acidified. As many as 15,000 lakes in eastern Canada are so acidic that they no longer contain fish.

The health effects of acid rain are more questionable. Acid in drinking water can certainly mobilize toxic metals, many of which cause neurological diseases. And acid air may impair breathing in individuals whose lungs are already diseased with illnesses like emphysema or asthma. But the extent of its effects on healthy people is still controversial. Researchers at the Mount Sinai School of Medicine in New York City contend that acid rain may be the third most important cause of lung disease, after smoking and passive smoking. A congressional study has blamed acid rain for contributing to more than 50,000 premature deaths in the U.S. and Canada each year, and a study at Harvard Medical School has linked it to 100,000 deaths per year. Other researchers, however, label such findings sheer speculation.

Sulfur dioxide is released into the air in the burning of sulfur-containing coal and petroleum. Nitrogen oxides are produced during the burning of most fuels, particularly when combustion occurs at high temperatures. Unlike the problem of air pollution, acid rain is not localized. Sulfur and nitrogen oxides released from tall smokestacks can travel hundreds of miles before being converted to acid rain. Most acid rain in Canada, for example, comes from the U.S., while that in Scandinavian countries comes from Central Europe.

Most efforts to reduce acid rain must be initiated by governments or public utilities. The simplest measure involves substituting low-sulfur fuels for those containing higher amounts of sulfur. Other options include removing sulfur from coal or oil before it is burned or using "precipitators" in smokestacks that remove sulfur dioxide from the exhaust gases. These approaches are, however, expensive.

The green consumer's primary contribution to reducing acid rain is to consume less electricity by eliminating unnecessary use and purchasing high-efficiency appliances. Acidic emissions from automobiles and trucks can also be reduced by purchasing cars that have good gas mileage, keeping them tuned up, keeping tires properly inflated, and keeping catalytic converters in proper operating condition so that output of nitrogen oxides is minimized.

Batteries

Batteries are a growing pollution source in the U.S. and other countries because they contain **mercury**, a cause of damage to the brain and nervous system, and cadmium, a cause of kidney damage. Batteries also contain smaller quantities of other toxic metals. Mercury is used in most types of batteries to prevent corrosion at the terminals, but especially in the newer button-shape type found in watches, calculators, and other electronic gadgets. By some estimates, the manufacture of batteries accounts for 50 percent of all mercury used each year in the U.S. and 25 percent of the cadmium.

In improperly designed landfills, mercury and other metals leach out and contaminate groundwater when batteries corrode. This has been a particular problem in Japan, where large numbers of batteries are used each year, and where **landfills** are usually not lined with plastic to prevent toxic chemicals from leaching out. The button-shape batteries also represent a problem because infants and children often swallow them. The batteries can cause inflammation and burn holes in the intestines, but so far are not believed to have caused any deaths.

It is unlikely that consumers will stop using batteries, but it may become necessary for batteries to be separated from other household trash and sent to special recycling or disposal plants. Some communities already separate batteries from trash, recycle their metals, and bury what's left in hazardous waste landfills.

The green consumer might consider using rechargeable batteries. Despite their high initial cost, they minimize pollution. These batteries, however, must also be disposed of eventually, and they do contain cadmium.

Automobile batteries are another major disposal problem because of the high quantities of toxic **lead** they contain. About two-thirds of the lead used in the U.S. goes to the manufacture of car batteries, and about 80 million such batteries are discarded each year. Although lead-acid batteries can be recycled, most are simply dumped in landfills. Acid leaks out and dissolves materials around it before escaping into groundwater. There, lead also dissolves and it can contaminate water. Some communities now require deposits on new batteries to ensure that they will be returned for proper recycling. The green consumer never discards car batteries in the trash, but instead returns them to a store or service station that will send them to a recycling center.

Biodegradation

The term "biodegradation" refers to the process by which paper, lawn sweepings, garbage, and other organic materials (made by or from living organisms) are broken down by microorganisms in the soil into innocuous materials, primarily methane (natural gas), carbon dioxide, and water. The process can occur in materials lying on the ground, buried, or immersed in water, but it occurs most efficiently in compost heaps, where the heat generated by bacterial activity accelerates the process.

In theory, organic materials should decompose readily in the **landfills** used for disposal of **solid waste**. In practice, however, biodegradation in most landfills is very limited. Researchers excavating closed landfills after 15 to 25 years find intact food—recognizable hot dogs and sweet rolls, for example—readable newspapers, and other items.

The problem, most scientists agree, is that present landfills have been designed to keep out rainwater so that toxic materials do not seep into groundwater. But without water, biodegradation is severely impeded. By some estimates, less than a quarter of all organic materials in a landfill is destroyed in the first 50 years. Researchers hope to increase biodegradation primarily by adding water and recycling it throughout the fill. Such techniques can have an additional benefit: the methane produced in landfills by biodegradation can be trapped and burned as a fuel—a feat already being achieved in some landfill operations.

Most **plastics** are not biodegradable, since they cannot be eaten by microorganisms. One attempted solution is to combine part of the plastic with specially prepared starch. When bacteria and other microorganisms eat the starch, they break the plastic down into smaller pieces that can be further degraded by the elements. (Nevertheless, complete degradation never takes place—plastics are forever.) A biodegradable plastic made completely from starch has recently been developed, and plastics made by bacteria, that can be eaten by bacteria are also being developed.

But so-called biodegradable plastics are slightly more expensive than the conventional plastics they replace. They are not as strong and may decompose prematurely. Biodegradable plastics also cannot readily be recycled in combination with conventional plastics without substantially weakening the new products.

But, perhaps most important, biodegradable plastics simply do not decompose under the conditions currently found in most landfills, so their use provides little benefit. Environmental groups now consider biodegradable plastics little more than a marketing ploy that does not make any real contribution to the solid waste problem. And because of adverse effects on recycling, some groups even advocate boycotting companies that use biodegradable plastics. Among the products most commonly made from biodegradable plastics are grocery bags, disposable diapers, and trash bags.

The bottom line for the green consumer? Until truly biodegradable plastic bags become a reality, stick with paper bags whenever possible. Reduce the number of plastic bags you use by eliminating as many "disposable" items as possible and by reusing them, and try composting food scraps. (See Chapter 2, "The Kitchen," for a discussion of the merits of using recycled plastic bags in supermarkets.)

Chlorofluorocarbons (See Ozone Depletion)

Deforestation

Tropical rainforests occupy only about 2 percent of the earth's surface but they contain as many as 80 percent of the planet's species of plants, animals, and insects. About 2.5 acres of tropical forest can contain as many as 800 different species of trees, more than are found in the whole of North America. A 4-square-mile area can easily contain 1,500 different species of flowering plants, 125 different mammals, 400 kinds of birds, 100 reptiles, 60 amphibians, and countless insects. So far, only a small fraction of the many species in the rainforests have been identified and classified.

Many of the species may never get the chance to be identified. Humans are destroying rainforests at the rate of 50 acres per minute—an area equivalent to the state of Pennsylvania each year. About one-quarter of the deforestation is carried out by governments and industry as they cut roads into the areas, install hydroelectric dams, and perform wholesale logging. The majority of the deforestation is carried out by local ranchers, who cut down trees and burn them in order to provide pastures for their cattle herds or new farmland.

Slash-and-burn agriculture has a devastating effect on the land. In rainforests, virtually all the nutrients are in the plants themselves and in the top inch or so of soil. When the trees are cut and burned, many of the nutrients are washed away by rains. The rest are used up in the first two or three years of farming. By the end of the third year, agricultural productivity is reduced to perhaps 25 percent of what it was in the first year, and the rancher is forced to clear new areas of forest to plant his crops. As the forest disappears, an estimated 4,000 to 6,000 species of animals, plants, and insects become extinct each year.

The damage doesn't end there. When the forests are cut and the claylike soil is exposed to sunlight, it bakes into a rock-hard layer that is impervious to plants and water. And because of the heat released by this mud, the air becomes dryer, less rain falls, and average temperatures rise—the climate is changed substantially. Under the new conditions, the rainforest can never grow back, even when the land is abandoned. The damage is irreversible.

Why should the green consumer be concerned? For a variety of reasons. Slash-and-burn agriculture contributes as much as 20 percent of the carbon dioxide released into the atmosphere each year by humans, the major cause of **global warming**. Perhaps even more important is the loss of biodiversity—the disappearance of a host of valuable species. The estimated 80 million different species of life in the rainforests represent a vast storehouse of genetic information that could prove useful to humans in providing new sources of drugs, agricultural cross-breeding, and food itself.

The green consumer can take several actions to help limit deforestation. Avoid purchasing items made of tropical hardwoods, such as mahogany, ebony, and teak. Instead, choose woods from North American forests that are replaced after logging. These include ash, beech, birch, cherry, elm, hickory, oak, poplar, and black walnut.

Dioxins

Dioxins are a family of 75 closely related chemicals that are by-products of the manufacture of such products as herbicides, the disinfectant hexachlorophene, the wood preservative pentachlorophenol, and paper. They are also formed during the incineration of many materials, including **plastics** such as polyvinyl chloride, PCBs, wood treated with preservatives, and **lead**ed gasoline. Although many of the dioxins are relatively innocuous, those that contain large proportions of chlorine are dangerous. One of them, called TCDD, is believed to be the most toxic chemical produced by humans. When environmentalists and scientists discuss dioxins, they are usually talking about TCDD.

TCDD accumulates in fatty tissues and is toxic to animals in doses so small as to be almost beyond comprehension—toxic dosage is measured in parts per trillion (the equivalent of one drop of water in an Olympic-sized swimming pool). In even lower doses it causes birth defects, reproductive defects, and perhaps cancer. In humans, it also produces a disfiguring skin disease called chloracne. Most people have small amounts of dioxins in their tissues, from general environmental exposure. Some wild birds also have it in their flesh, as do fish taken from the Great Lakes, many rivers (especially those near manufacturing centers), and waterways downstream from paper mills.

Herbicides containing dioxins were banned in the U.S. in 1983, but more than one million pounds per year were used on grazing lands and certain food crops in preceding years. No one knows how much dioxin remains in the soil or is present in food crops grown in the soil. Dioxins were present in herbicides widely used during the Vietnam War, and Asian researchers have reported a threefold increase in birth defects in the regions sprayed. Dioxins have also been found as contaminants in oil sprayed on rural roads to keep dust down.

Dioxins are formed in papermills from the chlorine compounds used for converting pulp into paper and for bleaching paper. In 1989, the EPA found small quantities of dioxins in milk sold in paper cartons and in coffee filters. The EPA did not consider the quantities large enough to cause problems, but even so, the manufacturers of these products have since changed processes so that less dioxin is present. Extremely small amounts of dioxins are found in most white papers.

The best way to avoid dioxins is not to eat fish taken from the Great Lakes and from urban rivers. Exposure can also be minimized by making greater use of unbleached paper products, including towels and coffee filters.

Eutrophication

In eutrophication, large quantities of nutrients such as phosphates and nitrogen compounds in rivers and lakes promote excessive growth of algae. When the algae die, their decay consumes virtually all of the dissolved oxygen in the water, thereby suffocating fish, shellfish, and other desirable species and leaving behind an ecological void. Although sewage sludge is one cause of eutrophication, more important are the phosphates that were commonly used in the past in laundry detergents. The phosphates act as "builders" in detergents, keeping soil suspended in water so that it isn't redeposited on clothes.

Eutrophication was first brought to public attention in the 1960s, when foam-filled waterways throughout the country became nearly devoid of life and Lake Erie was considered virtually dead. Since then, many states and local communities have banned the use of phosphates in detergents. Manufacturers have also sharply reduced their use in detergents and have developed other builders to take their place. These, typically, either do not work as well as phosphates or present environmental problems of their own.

Global Warming (See Greenhouse Effect)

Greenhouse Effect

The glass panes of a greenhouse allow all the sun's warming radiation to enter the building, but block the escape of heat radiated by the soil. The trapped heat can easily make the inside temperature 20 to 30 degrees warmer than outside. The same phenomenon occurs in the atmosphere. So-called greenhouse gases allow sunlight to reach the Earth's surface, but prevent heat from being radiated back into space. Natural variations in the amount of greenhouse gases in the atmosphere are thought to have been the cause of wide variations in the Earth's temperature in the past.

Now, however, humans are beginning to add large quantities of greenhouse gases to the atmosphere, and scientists fear that the planet will warm irrevocably as a result. The Earth's average temperature is estimated to have risen about a degree since the beginning of the Industrial Revolution in the mid-1800s, and some projections indicate that the temperature could rise by as much as 8 degrees Fahrenheit by the year 2030.

Warming of the Earth's average temperature would produce a variety of effects, few of them beneficial. The primary growing regions of the world would shift northward. Long periods of hot weather in the U.S. would be more common, and droughts would affect the Midwest more frequently. Tropical storms, hurricanes, and monsoons would all increase in power, perhaps by as much as 50 percent. Changes in ocean circulation could disrupt food sources for many of the fish that are commercially harvested. And melting of the polar ice caps would cause sea levels to rise, flooding low-lying areas along the coasts and making some island nations simply disappear.

If, in a worst case scenario, ocean levels were to rise 15 feet—within the realm of possibility—most of Florida would be inundated and, in Washington, D.C., water would flood National Airport and the Lincoln Memorial, reaching nearly to the Capitol's steps.

The most important greenhouse gas is carbon dioxide, which is produced when fossil fuels and forests are burned. It is present naturally in the atmosphere only in minute quantities, but human beings release about 5.5

billion tons every year. The U.S. contributes about a quarter of that amount, an average of about 6 tons per person per year. Since 1850, the amount of carbon dioxide in the atmosphere has increased by about 50 percent, and researchers expect it to nearly double again within 100 years if we continue to burn fossil fuels.

Chlorofluorocarbons (see **Ozone Depletion**) are actually a much stronger greenhouse gas than carbon monoxide. One molecule of a chlorofluorocarbon can absorb as much heat as 10,000 molecules of carbon dioxide. Fortunately, chlorofluorocarbons are present in lower concentrations.

Methane, another greenhouse gas, is produced when bacteria decompose organic matter. Its most important sources are swamps, rice paddies, the rumens of cattle, and termite mounds in the tropics. Nitrogen oxides, a by-product of combustion and released from artificial fertilizers, are also greenhouse gases. Together, these three sources account for about 40 percent of the greenhouse effect now, and researchers believe they will account for 50 percent by the next century.

In the U.S. and most industrialized countries, about 35 percent of the carbon dioxide released into the atmosphere comes from production of electricity, 30 percent from cars and trucks, 24 percent from industry, and 11 percent from home heating. Every gallon of gas burned in a car produces 20 pounds of carbon dioxide. A car that averages 18 mpg puts out a ton of carbon dioxide every 1,800 miles, or a total of 57.75 tons over the course of its lifetime. In developing countries, a large proportion of the carbon dioxide arises from burning or the decay of trees cut down during **deforestation.**

Fuel choices are very important. Burning coal produces about one-third more carbon dioxide than burning petroleum, and about twice as much as burning natural gas. Both natural gas and petroleum cost more, however. Because such a large proportion of carbon dioxide comes from electricity production and transportation, the most important contribution a green consumer can make is to reduce energy use. That includes purchasing high-efficiency appliances and minimizing their unnecessary use.

High-efficiency automobiles are also helpful. A car that averages 50 mpg releases only 40 percent as much carbon dioxide as one that averages 20 mpg. Keep your car tuned and use radial tires to reduce friction and increase mileage efficiency. Finally, insulating homes can reduce the energy required for heating and thereby the amount of carbon dioxide produced.

Landfills (See Solid Waste)

Lead

Lead is an extremely toxic heavy metal. In adults, lead poisoning can cause kidney damage, injury to the central and peripheral nervous systems, and even brain damage in particularly aggravated cases. Exposure to lead before or during pregnancy can also lead to miscarriages. The damage to children is more insidious and occurs at much lower levels because of lead's effects on their developing brains and nervous systems. The metal can reduce a child's intelligence and cause hearing problems, hyperactivity, impaired reaction time, impulsiveness, and difficulty in persisting in a task. Experts say that as many as 17 percent of children in urban areas have a potentially dangerous level of lead in their blood.

The most common sources of lead in the environment are lead-containing paint, automobile exhaust from leaded fuels, and lead-emitting industries. Lead from discarded automobile **batteries** can also escape from **landfills** and contaminate water supplies.

Lead was widely used as a pigment in paints, until the mid-1950s, when manufacturers began phasing out its use. That use was largely prohibited by the Consumer Products Safety Commission in 1977, but lead-containing paints are still found in most houses built prior to the 1950s, especially on windows, trim, and doors.

Lead paint oxidizes slowly, releasing fine particles of lead oxide into the air. The paint can also peel or flake off and is sometimes eaten by children who are attracted to its sweet taste. One surprising source of lead poisoning in children is the process of urban gentrification. When people purchase older homes in cities and renovate them, the renovation process often releases lead particles, dust, and fumes into the air, where it can settle on toys, clothing, and other household objects. The problem is generally more severe in cases where the home owners do the renovations themselves.

Although leaded gasoline is being phased out of production, most soil in cities and in areas beside highways is contaminated with lead. Children playing in the soil unwittingly ingest significant amounts. The metal also appears in vegetables and fruit grown in backyard gardens in such areas. Lead pipes are common in older homes. Water flowing through the pipes can extract lead, particularly if the water is acidic, as is the case in areas that suffer from **acid rain.** In 1987, researchers also found lead in drinking water coming from many types of electric drinking fountains.

The green consumer can avoid most lead poisoning by using common sense. If your house has lead pipes or lead solder, use treatment devices to remove lead from water or run the cold tap for several minutes before drinking, particularly in the morning when water has been sitting in pipes all night; use bottled water for infants; do not drink hot tap water or cook with it (it dissolves more lead). In urban areas, plant grass or other groundcover to retard dust; turn soil over 12 to 18 inches deep after wetting down to contain dust; replace top layer with uncontaminated soil. Wear a face mask when doing this, cover up well, and wet down the soil before beginning.

To renovate old buildings, cover wall areas with a durable material like paneling or sheetrock; remove old paint only as a last resort. Replace doors, windows, and woodwork or send them to be chemically stripped. Store toys and clothes in dust-free areas during renovation and try to keep the children away during the work. Take particular care during cleanup. Most vacuum cleaners, for example, simply distribute lead more evenly through the house because small particles of lead dust pass easily through vacuum-cleaner bags. Use only a high-efficiency or water-based vacuum cleaner that is capable of trapping and holding the tiny particles. Also, wet-mop all areas to bind and hold lead particles. Finally, do not discard automobile batteries with household trash; take them to a service station that will send them to a recycling center.

Many experts recommend testing the levels of lead in the blood of certain groups of children because lead poisoning is often not initially apparent. In order of priority, those groups include: children, ages 9 months to 6 years, who live in or are frequent visitors in older, dilapidated buildings; children, ages 9 months to 6 years, who are siblings, housemates, visitors, or playmates of children with known lead toxicity; children who live near lead smelters and processing plants; children whose parents or other household members participate in a lead-related occupation or hobby; and children, ages 9 months to 6 years, who live near highways with heavy traffic.

Microwaves

Microwave radiation, a form of **electromagnetic radiation,** can cause cataracts among individuals exposed to it for even short periods. The heating effects of microwaves can also be damaging to living cells and organisms. Most microwaves designed for home and industrial use are properly shielded so that such radiation does not escape. If you are concerned, however, have a service person check for stray radiation.

Ozone Depletion

When you relax on the beach for several hours or play a game of baseball in the bright sunlight, you may turn red from sunburn. That burn is caused by ultraviolet light, a component of sunlight. Ultraviolet light has a wavelength that is too long to be perceived by human eyesight, but with sufficient energy to badly damage cells exposed to it, even to the point of causing them to become cancerous.

Fortunately 99 percent of the sun's ultraviolet light is screened out before it reaches the earth's surface by a wispy layer of a gas called ozone. (Ozone formed at ground level is a major contributor to **air pollution,** combining with other chemicals in the air to form **smog**. This ozone is too heavy to reach the upper atmosphere.)

Many gases produced on the Earth's surface can float up to the upper levels of the atmosphere where they destroy ozone, exerting an effect far out of proportion to their actual concentration. The most important of these ozone destroyers are a family of chemicals called chlorofluorocarbons or CFCs, a gaseous relative of the nonstick Teflon surfaces found on cookware.

CFCs, often known by the trade name Freon, are highly inert chemicals: they don't burn, are non-toxic to humans, cannot be consumed by bacteria, and are not destroyed by chemical processes on the Earth's surface. Because of these properties, as well as their chemical characteristics, they are widely used in industry, most commonly as refrigerants. They are also used as a blowing agent to produce insulating gas pockets in plastic foams like those used in fast-food containers and home insulation. The microelectronics industry uses CFCs as a solvent to cleanse solder residues and other materials from printed circuit boards. And they are still used in some parts of the world as a propellant for spray cans.

When the CFCs escape into the atmosphere—by leaking from auto air conditioners or abandoned refrigerators, by seeping out of plastic foams, or by simply evaporating from electronics factories—they float up to the highest reaches of the atmosphere. There, sunlight breaks them apart, freeing the chemicals that destroy ozone. Scientists estimate that enough CFCs have already been released into the atmosphere to reduce the ozone layer by 5 to 10 percent by early in the next century. Already, scientists believe, the ozone layer has been depleted by an average of about 2 percent around the world and, in certain areas, by much more. Over Antarctica, the concentration of ozone drops by as much as 50 percent during the three-month spring, producing the so-called ozone-hole. A similar hole has recently been found over the Arctic, but the extent of depletion in that region during winter is still only about 15 percent.

The increased ultraviolet light reaching the Earth's surface as a result of long-term ozone depletion is expected to cause a marked increase in the incidence of skin cancer among people who work or spend a large amount of time outdoors. Some evidence suggests it will impair immunity as well. It will also kill plankton and algae in the ocean's surface, important microorganisms in the ocean's food chain. The production of agricultural crops will probably also be affected.

After a long and bitter dispute, consensus was finally reached in 1989 that CFCs are destroying significant amounts of ozone and that measures should be taken to stop their production and use. By June 1990, 92 countries had agreed to an international protocol that would eliminate all uses of CFCs by January 1, 2000. Thirteen of the countries, including Canada, Sweden, and West Germany (but not the United States), agreed to eliminate all uses of the chemicals by 1997.

One early step in the U.S. was a ban on the use of CFCs in spray cans in 1978. Another obvious target is the foam containers used to package fast foods and takeout orders.

Although these containers help keep food warm, they are not necessary: some fast-food chains have always used cardboard containers.

Manufacturers are developing alternatives to CFCs, typically compounds that are closely related, but that can be degraded in the lower atmosphere. Before these compounds can be widely used, however, their potential toxicity must be determined. Moreover, because these materials are less efficient than CFCs, new refrigerators and air conditioners will typically be larger and heavier and, perhaps, require more electricity. Automobiles with air conditioners will have slightly lower fuel efficiency and get lower mileage per gallon.

For the moment, the green consumer has only a few ways to directly affect the ozone problem. Patronize take-out restaurants that use only cardboard containers or foam containers labeled as being CFC-free (although the current CFC-free containers are not necessarily an environmental bargain since they are not yet recyclable). Also avoid using foam coffee cups, virtually all of which are still made with CFCs. Buying a car without an air conditioner is probably not a realistic option for many people, but one state, Vermont, has forbidden the sale of such vehicles. (Obviously, it's easier for Vermont than for Arizona).

Several companies have developed techniques to recycle CFCs. When a refrigerator or air conditioner is repaired, such companies can capture and clean the CFCs for reuse instead of venting them into the atmosphere. Ask your automobile dealer or repair person if they recycle; if they don't, try to find someone who does.

A few other chemicals also adversely affect the ozone layer. These include halons, which are used to suppress fires in electronic installations and military vehicles. They are also found in many fire extinguishers.

Nitrogen oxides emitted directly into the upper atmosphere by supersonic aircraft also are a problem. By one estimate, a commercial fleet of supersonic craft could do as much damage to the ozone layer as CFCs.

Ozone depletion is not subject to a "technological fix," such as the release of more ozone into the upper atmosphere. The energy in the sunlight that converts oxygen into ozone in a one-hour period is equal to all the energy produced on Earth during one year. Clearly, anything that could be done by humans to improve the situation is insignificant in comparison.

Packaging

Last year, materials used in packaging consumer goods accounted for about 105 billion pounds of solid wastes, about one-third of the total weight of material directed to **landfills**. That packaging consists primarily of paper (48 percent), glass (27 percent), and **plastics** (11 percent). The proportion accounted for by plastics is growing rapidly, however, primarily because of the increased sales of prepackaged convenience foods, especially those designed for use in microwave ovens. The proportion of plastics in municipal solid waste is expected to grow from 7 percent in 1987 to 10 percent in the year 2000, increasing from 22 billion pounds to 38 billion pounds.

A growing percentage of cardboard and paper packaging uses recycled paper, a major environmental improvement. Recycling paper requires 60 percent less energy and 15 percent less water than the production of virgin paper. It also saves trees and reduces the need for landfills. For virtually all applications, recycled paper is every bit as good as virgin paper.

Pesticides

American farmers use 1.5 billion pounds of pesticides every year, about five pounds for every man, woman, and child in the country, in addition to 560 million pounds of herbicides and fungicides. Critics charge that the pesticides produce little benefit. At the beginning of the century when pesticides were virtually unheard of, farmers lost about one-third of their crops to pests. Today, despite the widespread use of pesticides, farmers still lose about one-third of their crops to pests, largely because pests have developed resistance to the most commonly used pesticides.

In 1938 etymologists knew of just 7 species of insects and mites that were resistant to pesticides. Today there are at least 447 and the number is growing. Herbicide use has also created an unknown number of "superweeds" that can no longer be controlled chemically. As a result of this increased resistance to both pesticides and herbicides, researchers are continually developing newer and more lethal varieties whose potential health effects are largely unknown. The EPA says that at least 66 pesticides used on American food crops are known to cause cancer, as do about 60 percent of the fungicides and herbicides. According to the agency, at least 74 different pesticides have been found in the groundwater of 38 states.

The average home owner uses 5 to 10 pounds of pesticides and herbicides on his lawn each year, about 10 times as much toxic chemicals per acre as farmers use. Often, the home owner will then saturate the lawn with water, washing the pesticides (and also fertilizers) straight into sewers, septic systems, and rivers. Pesticides and fertilizers from home use are one of the major sources of water pollution (see **Pollution, Water**) in the U.S. Many experts believe that home use of pesticides also endangers many species of songbirds by contaminating the worms they eat.

A small but growing number of farmers and home owners are turning toward alternative methods of pest management, such as "low-impact farming" and integrated pest management. These farmers use only the minimum amount of chemicals necessary to maintain productivity, supplementing them with alternative techniques that rely more on natural predators of the pests, crop rotation, and using pesticides isolated from natural sources.

Photodegradation

Photodegradation is the destruction of materials by the ultraviolet light in sunlight. When newspapers are left out in sunlight, for example, they darken and eventually fall apart. Most **plastics** are also degraded by sunlight, but only very slowly. That process can be accelerated by incorporating molecules susceptible to damage by ultraviolet light within the plastic molecules, thus reducing the size of the plastic molecules so they can be further decomposed by microorganisms.

Because neither neon nor tungsten light bulbs produce ultraviolet light and window glass absorbs it, photodegradable plastics last indefinitely on store shelves, but begin to break down when they are exposed to sunlight. The speed with which they decompose can be tailored from a few weeks to a few years.

When buried in a **landfill,** of course, the photodegradable plastics do not break down because they are not exposed to light, and therefore add to the solid waste problem. The plastic rings that hold together six-packs of sodas, for example, are a severe hazard to wildlife. They strangle and disfigure fish, birds, and other animals that become entangled in them, and prevent them from eating when the rings encircle their heads or necks. Photodegraable plastics are one solution to this problem; within a few days, they become weak enough for animals to break free (assuming that the animal can survive that long). At least 17 states now require that the plastic rings be photodegradable, and a Federal law scheduled to take effect in 1991 requires that all such loops be photodegradable.

Most other current and potential uses of photodegradable plastics have less direct impact on the consumer—for example, the large plastic fishing nets now used by commercial fishermen. When these nets are damaged, fishing boats simply cut them loose. The nets float in the ocean, continuing to trap and kill fish—a process known as "ghost fishing"—or becoming entangled in the propellers of other ships. The use of photodegradable nets would alleviate both these problems. Photodegradable plastic films are also being used as mulch on commercial crops to hold moisture in soil, reduce weed growth, and prevent nutrient runoff. Conventional plastic films must be removed during the growing season and taken to landfills at a cost of perhaps $100 per acre. Photodegradable mulch simply disappears from sight although tiny plastic molecules remain in the soil.

Plasticizers

When your car is parked in sunlight for long periods of time, a thin film builds up on the inside of windows, partially obscuring vision. This film is composed of plasticizers that are added to floor coverings, plastic wrap, plastic-coated wallpapers, paints, lacquers, toys, nipples on baby bottles and pacifiers, and vinyl seat covers to make them softer and more flexible. Plasticizers are not chemically bonded to the plastics, so they can migrate to the surface where they evaporate into the air. Because they are released from all these sources, plasticizers are virtually ubiquitous in the environment.

Like DDT and many other large organic molecules, the plasticizers tend to accumulate in fats, and thus can persist in the body for long periods of time. Researchers have, however, reached few conclusions about the health effects. Unfortunately, whatever the risk, there does not seem to be any way for the green consumer to avoid contact with the materials.

Plastics

Plastics are composed of long-chain molecules, called "polymers," and are generally made from petroleum. The long molecules cannot be consumed by microorganisms, which makes plastics virtually indestructible in normal use and when they are buried in **landfills.** Ironically, the low cost of plastics has led to their wide use in disposable items made to be used once—often for no more than a couple of minutes—and then thrown away. Each year American manufacturers produce about 10 pounds of plastics for every person on the Earth. That development has contributed to the growing **solid waste** problem in the U.S.; some 20 to 30 percent of the wastes in landfills, by volume, are plastics.

Plastics fall into two main categories, thermoplastics and thermosets. Thermoplastic materials soften without degrading when they are heated and thus can be recycled into new products. Thermoset plastics degrade when they are heated and cannot be recycled. One good example of thermosets is the plastic used in Thermos bottles.

Thermoplastics come in a variety of types that have different properties and different uses:

- ◆ Polyethylene (PE): About 47 percent of plastics used in the U.S., its major applications include milk jugs, garbage bags, grocery bags, and most liquid soap and detergent bottles.

- ◆ Polypropylene (PP): Sixteen percent of plastics are PP. It is used in some electric appliances, videocassette cases, drinking straws, and screw-on caps.

- ◆ Polystyrene (PS): This also accounts for 16 percent. It is used mainly for foam cups, plates, and hamburger containers, plastic utensils, and radio and television cabinets.

- ◆ Polyvinyl chloride (PVC): 6.5 percent of plastics are PVC. It is a very tough plastic used in plumbing pipe, plastic wrap, and clear containers.

- ◆ Polyethylene terephthalate (PET): This accounts for only 5 percent, but is one of the fastest growing. Its main use is in soda bottles and in other clear containers, such as salad oil bottles.

- ◆ Polyurethane: This also accounts for 5 percent of plastics and is used for foam insulation, floor finishing, and cushions.

All these plastics can be recycled. In fact, manufacturers routinely recycle virtually 100 percent of their scraps left over from production. The main task in recycling plastics is to separate them from other trash and separate the different plastics from one another. This is accomplished by chopping the waste into small pieces and separating the plastics by density. Some manufacturers have also begun labeling plastic bottles so that they can easily be separated manually. Some products, like squeezable ketchup bottles, are made of several different plastics laminated together in such a manner that they cannot be separated. These products cannot be recycled.

Pollution, Air

Air pollution takes a variety of forms, ranging from the acidic materials that form **acid rain** to toxic chemicals emitted by industrial plants. Nearly half of all Americans, an estimated 110 million, live in areas with what the EPA considers air unhealthy at least part of the time.

The EPA has identified 320 different toxic chemicals in city air, but the most important forms of air pollution are smog and carbon monoxide. Carbon monoxide is formed from the incomplete combustion of organic fuels, particularly gasoline in automobiles and wood in stoves. It is poisonous at high concentrations, interfering with the ability of hemoglobin in the blood to carry oxygen. At lower concentrations, it can cause asthma, emphysema, and other chronic obstructive lung diseases. Denver, in particular, has a serious carbon monoxide problem in winter because the high altitude and cold air combine to reduce the amount of oxygen available to combine with fuels during combustion.

Smog is usually a summer problem. A combination of smoke, fog, and other pollutants, it occurs when nitrogen oxides and unburned hydrocarbons combine in sunlight to produce ozone and other noxious chemicals. The nitrogen oxides come from cars and stationary combustion sources. The hydrocarbons come from the same sources, as well as from aerosol containers, charcoal lighter, dry-cleaning fluid, and a host of other sources.

Each month the residents of the Los Angeles basin release into the air an amount of hydrocarbons equivalent to the oil spilled by the Exxon Valdez. Smog is frequently made worse by so-called inversion layers—a blanket of cold air over a city that traps warm air underneath it and all the pollutants with it. Smog injures the lungs, damages buildings, lowers agricultural yields, and kills trees and other plants.

The green consumer can take a variety of steps to minimize smog formation. The most important is to own a high-mileage car, keep it tuned up, keep the catalytic converter in good operating condition, use radial tires, and keep tires properly inflated. Public transportation, when available, is an even better alternative.

Green consumers should reduce their use of electricity as much as possible, because emissions from generating plants are a major pollutant source. Natural gas water heaters should be kept in good repair. In many areas where smog is severe, more drastic measures are necessary and will eventually be mandated. Charcoal lighter fluid will be prohibited, for example, as will some types of aerosol cans and oil-based paints, which emit hydrocarbons while drying. Dry-cleaning plants will also be required to install new and safer equipment.

Pollution, Air, Indoor

Indoor air pollution is a growing problem, particularly as houses and commercial buildings are tightly sealed to minimize energy consumption. People are exposed to much higher levels of dangerous air pollutants in such buildings than they are outdoors, even in heavily industrialized cities. Indoor air pollution has so far been linked primarily to short-term health effects, but some of the chemicals found indoors are believed to cause cancer. The most common symptoms include headache, depression, irritation, fatigue, dry throat, sinus congestion, dizziness, and nausea. Physicians typically have a very difficult time identifying the problem.

Indoor air pollution typically arises from two different sources: microorganisms and toxic chemicals. Mold, bacteria, and fungi growing in heating, ventilation, and cooling systems in commercial buildings, cause a variety of allergic reactions. The microorganism that causes Legionaire's Disease is also released into the air by cooling systems.

Ironically, EPA headquarters in Washington, D.C., is a prime example of the so-called sick-building syndrome: workers there have come down with a variety of ailments that have been linked directly to pollutants in the building. Such ailments have also been identified in hospitals, schools, and nursing homes.

Toxic chemicals are probably a more severe source of indoor air pollution. Cleaning solvents, photocopying machine chemicals, and pesticides are typical sources of chemicals, but many also come from unexpected sources, including carpets, furniture, plywood, wallboard, latex caulk, adhesives, latex paint, telephone cable, and particle board. All contain a variety of volatile organic chemicals that evaporate and contaminate the air, particularly in the first few months after installation.

In the first few months of a building's occupation, indoor air should not be recycled, but should be replaced with fresh air from outside. If possible, do not keep a new house closed up during the first weeks of occupancy; allow time to air it out thoroughly so that all volatile chemicals can escape from furnishings.

The simplest way to determine if indoor contaminants are causing health problems is to move out briefly. Stay with a friend or relative for a few days and see if your symptoms subside. If they do, and then return when you move back into the house, it may be necessary to contact an environmental medicine specialist to determine how to cure the problem.

Pollution, Water

Waste discharges from industrial facilities and municipal sewage treatment plants are regulated under the 1972 Clean Water Act, and great reductions have been achieved—so much so that the bulk of water pollution in the U.S. now comes from what is called non-point-source pollution. That is a catchall term for contaminated runoff from a large number of miscellaneous sources, rather than, for example, from the pipe of an industrial facility or sewage treatment plant. Pollutants such as fertilizers and pesticides from farmers' fields and residential lawns, sediments from eroding fields, ditches, and construction sites, and toxic pollutants from urban areas are responsible for 76 percent of the water pollution in lakes, 65 percent in rivers, and 45 percent in estuaries. Non-point-source pollution is the most difficult source of water pollution to regulate, but it is also what the green consumer is most able to affect.

Most such pollution is carried to waterways in runoff from rain and snow. Home owners should therefore limit their use of fertilizers and pesticides. Motor oil, antifreeze, pesticides, paints, and other toxic chemicals should never be poured into gutters, storm sewers, catch basins, ditches, or drains. Ideally, they should be taken to a proper disposal facility. Similarly, to reduce nutrient and pathogens in runoff, grass trimmings, leaves, and other debris should never be placed in sewers—compost them or put them in the trash.

Radon

Radon is a colorless, odorless gas formed during the decay of uranium. Although it undergoes radioactive decay, emitting alpha particles that can damage cells, it is not generally considered hazardous because it is expelled from the lungs nearly as quickly as it is breathed in. But the elements produced during its decay, primarily radioactive isotopes of polonium, lead, and bismuth, are dangerous because they react chemically with airborne dust and smoke particles. These then can lodge in the lung for long periods of time and can produce cancer. The EPA estimates that at least 10,000 people, and perhaps as many as 20,000, die from lung cancer each year as a result of exposure to these products of radon decay.

Most soil contains small amounts of uranium and thus releases radon continuously; granite contains larger amounts. Outdoors, the radon is dispersed quickly, but it seeps into homes through dirt floors, cracks in walls and floors, floor drains, and sumps. It can build up to much higher levels, particularly in winter when the house is closed up. Houses that have been well insulated and highly weatherized often have the most severe problems.

Homes containing high levels of radon have been found in every state.

Home owners can test for radon by using commercial detectors or hiring contractors. For owner testing, the cost usually ranges from $20 to $50. Testing should be conducted in the winter, preferably over a period of several months. EPA's recommended limit for radon in homes is 4 picocuries per liter of air. If testing reveals a higher level, sealing cracks in floors and walls and installing ventilating fans may be sufficient to remove excess buildup. In more severe cases, it may be necessary to install special exhaust pipes to collect radon and vent it back outdoors. That may cost as much as $5,000.

Radon is less a green issue than one of personal health. Most nonsmoking Americans have a lifetime lung cancer risk of about one in 100. Living in a house with 10 picocuries of radon per liter increases the risk to a chance between 3 and 12 per 100. If the level is 100 picocuries per liter, the risk ranges to between 27 and 63 in 100.

Recycling

By some estimates, more than 50 percent of the **solid waste** that now goes into **landfills** could be recycled into useful products at a substantial savings in energy and raw materials costs. But only about 10 percent, primarily newspapers and aluminum cans, are now recycled through community recycling centers across the country.

In 1988, according to the Aluminum Association, Americans recycled 42.5 billion aluminum beverage cans, about 55 percent of the cans produced. The amount of aluminum that is thrown away every three months is enough to rebuild the U.S.'s entire fleet of commercial jet aircraft. Recycling aluminum is very simple: it is cleaned, melted, and reformed into new cans, a process that consumes only 5 percent as much energy as making a can from bauxite ore and produces only 5 percent as much pollution. New cans can be on store shelves in as little as six weeks. Recyclers like aluminum cans because they are easy to work with and highly profitable. Aluminum can be recycled an indefinite number of times, with only a small amount lost each time.

Americans use an estimated 67 million tons of paper annually, the equivalent of a forest of about 850 million trees. Sunday newspapers alone consume 500,000 trees every week. About one-quarter of all paper is recycled in the U.S., representing a savings of 200 million trees. Producing one ton of paper from waste papers uses 64 percent less energy and 58 percent less water than producing it from trees, and produces 74 percent less air pollution and 35 percent less water pollution. Cardboard is the most commonly recycled form of paper, with newspapers a close second.

Other types of paper should also be recycled. Americans receive about 2 million tons of junk mail each year, and nearly half of it is not opened or not read. Much of this paper could be recycled. Better yet, the green consumer can have his or her name removed from mailing lists by writing to: Mail Preference Service, Direct Marketing Association, P.O. Box 3861, New York, N.Y. 10163-3861. If a million people stopped their junk mail, it would save about 1.5 million trees each year. The average office worker also uses about one pound of paper per day, which could also be recycled. Currently, recycling companies pay significantly more for high-quality office paper than they do for newspapers, so companies can both reduce the costs of trash disposal and produce income by recycling.

Because of its composition, paper can be recycled only a finite number of times. During the recycling process, fibers in paper are broken down into weaker, shorter fibers. Recycled paper is therefore not appropriate for grocery bags because it tears too easily, nor can it usually be made as white as virgin paper.

Currently, the increased collection of paper for recycling has overwhelmed demand, and recyclers are paying only about half as much for newspapers as they were before. Some eastern communities have warehouses full of newspapers for which there is currently no market.

Glass bottles can also be readily recycled, but most are not. Americans throw away as many as 28 billion glass bottles and jars each year, enough to fill the twin towers of the New York's World Trade Center every two weeks. Some types of bottles, such as returnable soda bottles, can be reused by simply washing and refilling. In most cases, however, paper is removed and the glass is broken into small particles called "cullet." The cullet is then mixed with virgin glass to produce new bottles. Because cullet melts at lower temperatures than the materials used to make virgin glass, recycling requires about 32 percent less energy, and produces about 20 percent less air pollution and 50 percent less water pollution. Despite the ease with which glass can be recycled, however, communities with active recycling programs currently have a surplus of glass bottles, and in some cases have even been forced to dump them in landfills.

Most **plastics** can be recycled. Polyethylene terephthalate (PET) can be transformed into geotextiles for use in lining landfills, fiberfill for stuffing pillows and furniture, bathtubs, shower stalls, boat hulls, and carpets. Proctor & Gamble has developed a way to use recycled PET for bottles for its "Spic and Span" cleanser, and other companies are developing similar containers.

High-density polyethylene (HDPE) can be recycled into garden furniture, plastic fencing, flowerpots, and drainage pipes. And polyvinyl chloride (PVC) is used for drainage and sewer pipes, vinyl floor tiles, truck-bed liners, and downspouts. Some types of recycled plastic products can be turned into car stops, speed bumps, traffic cones, and plastic "lumber" suitable for benches, picnic tables, and other nonstructural uses.

One major impediment to increased recycling of plastics is the FDA's refusal to allow recycled materials to be used for packaging food and drinks for fear of contamination by microorganisms.

Another candidate for recycling is motor oil. Americans use about 1.2 billion gallons of motor oil each year, and as much as 35 percent of it winds up in the environment—dumped into sewers or onto soil. Up to 40 percent of the pollution in rivers may be caused by motor oil dumped into sewers. Oil dumped on the ground seeps into groundwater and pollutes it; one quart of oil can contaminate many thousands of gallons of drinking water.

Many communities have curbside programs for collecting used motor oils. Others have designated service stations that collect it for recycling for a small fee. Although the oil is typically contaminated with a variety of heavy metals produced by engine wear, it can be refined and reused as motor oil. With the use of additives, it can be converted to lubricating oil, and larger amounts can be burned as fuel for ships and industrial boilers. Recycled oil is also used in wood preservatives and as an ingredient in artificial fire logs.

Yet another automotive product, tires, can also be recycled. Every year, Americans discard as many as 260 million automobile tires. Many are placed in landfills where they trap gases and float to the surface. Others accumulate in used tire dumps, which frequently catch on fire, spewing toxic smoke into the air and toxic chemicals into the ground and groundwater. One way to recycle tires is to have them retreaded, a once-popular option that has increasingly fallen into disfavor. The rubber in the tires can also be put to a variety of uses, including adhesives, wire and pipe insulation, brake linings, conveyer belts, carpet padding, tractor tires, hoses, and as a component of asphalt.

Batteries can also be recycled readily if they are separated from other trash. Steel can be recycled as well, with substantial savings in energy and pollution, but some 70 percent of all steel products made in the U.S. are used just once, then discarded. At least 3 million automobiles are discarded every year, and most simply rust away in junkyards or by the side of the road.

Most experts agree that increased recycling will require government intervention. Many communities already require curbside recycling, in which newspapers, aluminum cans, and plastic and glass bottles are separated from the rest of the trash. Government can also encourage recycling by providing tax breaks for companies participating in recycling and easing some rules that now favor virgin materials over recycled.

Smog (See Pollution, Air)

Solid Waste

Every day each American produces about three pounds of trash, a total of about 158 millions tons per year, enough to fill the New Orleans Superdome completely twice per day, every day. EPA estimates that this amount will increase by about 20 percent by the year 2000. About 10 percent of this trash is recycled and perhaps as much as 5 percent is burned in municipal incinerators, but the rest is simply buried in **landfills,** which are quickly filling to capacity.

At least 500 new landfills are required every year simply

to keep even with trash production but, according to the Natural Resources Defense Council, the U.S. has 30 percent fewer landfills than it did in 1984. As many as one-third of all existing landfills are expected to close within five years and, in many cases, new sites are unavailable.

Some cities, such as Los Angeles, are contemplating hauling trash into the desert by train, while eastern cities like New York are eyeing sites in other states. Environmentalists generally object to such plans for long distance transport of solid wastes. (See the **Plastics** and **Biodegradation** entries for more information relating to landfill composition.)

The Green
Label Reader

T HIS SECTION LISTS the major chemical ingredients found in many common household items. Some of these items have no known environmental or health effects. Many of them are health hazards and should be used cautiously. Moreover, what's bad for you is generally bad for the environment. Most of the substances are volatile, so they contribute to air pollution. Pouring them down the drain contributes to the burden of organic materials in sewage. It also exposes wildlife to their harmful effects.

You can use this reader as you shop, so you'll know the environmental health affects of your potential purchases. You can also use it to develop your own set of "personal environmental health" standards for selecting household products. Either way, arm yourself with the knowledge you need to make informed buying decisions.

Substance	Use	Known Environmental/Health Effect
Ammonia	Degreasing agent, cleaner	Short exposures irritating to mucous membranes of nose, throat, and lungs. Prolonged exposure causes edema of respiratory tract, suffocation.
Ammonium hydroxide	Detergent, stain remover, bleaching agent	Releases ammonia.
Aluminosilicates	Water softener	None
Benzene	Solvent for waxes, resins, oils, paints, etc.	Acutely toxic: irritation of mucous membranes, restlessness, convulsions, respiratory failure; prolonged exposure can cause leukemia.
o-Benzyl-p-chlorophenol (chlorophene)	Disinfectant	Similar to phenol (see below).
Bisulfites	Preservative in foods and wines	Strong, occasionally fatal allergic reactions in sensitive people.
Butyldiglycol	Disinfectant	None
Calcium propionate	Mold inhibitor, preservative	None
Cetrimonium bromide	Detergent, antiseptic	None
Colors	Various dyes are used in foods and drugs, among others	Many dyes carcinogenic to mice in large quantities.
Cresol	Disinfectant, antiseptic	Digestive disturbances, nervous disorders, mental changes, skin eruptions, jaundice.
Diethanolamine	Emulsifier, dispersant, detergent	None
Dimethylbenzylammonium chloride	Disinfectant	None
Dyes (See Colors)		

Substance	Use	Known Environmental/Health Effect
Ethylene glycol monobutyl ether (Butyl Cellosolve)	Solvent, degreaser	See Methyl Cellosolve.
EDTA	Antioxidant, flavoring agent	Mobilizes toxic metals in drinking water; potential groundwater contaminant.
Formaldehyde	Disinfectant, germicide, preservative	Skin irritation, anemia; higher doses cause vertigo, coma, death; prolonged exposure causes cancer.
Fragrance	Term for thousands of ingredients that compose odors	Allergic reactions; adds organic chemicals to sewage.
Glycerin (glycerol)	Solvent, sweetener, emollient, plasticizer	None
Hydroxyacetic acid (glycolic acid)	Adhesives, copper brightening, cleaning metals	Irritates skin and mucous membranes.
Isopropyl alcohol (isopropanol)	Disinfectant, antiseptic, solvent	Ingested or inhaled: flushing, dizziness, headache, depression, nausea, vomiting, coma.
Methyl Cellosolve	Solvent in nail polishes, quick-drying varnishes, enamels, wood stains	Ingested or inhaled: anemia, disorders of central nervous system.
Mineral oil	Solvent, emollient	Suspected carcinogen, interferes with vitamin absorption if swallowed.
Morpholine	Solvent for resins, waxes	Irritating to eyes, skin, mucous membranes.
MSG (monosodium glutamate)	Flavor enhancer	May cause "Chinese Restaurant Syndrome"—numbness, weakness, heart palpitations, headache.
Naphthalene	Insecticide, antiseptic, moth repellent	Ingested or inhaled: nausea, vomiting, headache; more significant exposure can lead to convulsions or coma.

Substance	Use	Known Environmental/Health Effect
Nitrates	Preservative, antioxidant	When nitrates are converted in the body into nitrites: can cause low blood pressure, headache, vertigo, nausea, diarrhea; also converted into carcinogenic nitrosamines in the digestive tract.
Nitrites	Preservative, antioxidant	See Nitrates.
Nitrobenzene	Used in soaps, shoe polishes	Ingested or inhaled: headaches, drowsiness, nausea, vomiting; larger quantities can cause blood disorders.
Oleic acid	Lubricant, in polishing compounds, solvent	Mildly irritating to skin, mucous membranes.
Oxalic acid	In metal polishes, wood cleaners; paint, varnish and rust removers.	Caustic and corrosive to skin and mucous membranes; ingested: nausea, vomiting, diarrhea; larger quantities can cause convulsions, coma, death.
Paradichlorobenzene	Insecticidal fumigant	Irritation to skin, throat, eyes; with prolonged exposure to high concentrations: weakness, dizziness, loss of weight, liver injury.
Perchloroethylene (tetrachloroethylene)	Degreasing agent, solvent, drycleaning fluid	Removes fats from skin, causing dermatitis; narcotic in high concentrations.
Pentachlorophenol	Insecticide, herbicide, wood preservative	Can impair breathing, lower blood pressure; causes lung, liver, and kidney damage; motor weakness; with higher exposures: convulsions or death.
Petroleum distillates (See Petroleum naphtha)		
Petroleum naphtha	Solvent	Defatting of skin causes irritation, infection; inhaled: drowsiness, headache, coma; ingested: vomiting and diarrhea.

Substance	Use	Known Environmental/Health Effect
Phenol	Disinfectant	Nausea, vomiting; larger quantities: circulatory collapse, paralysis, convulsions, coma, death.
o-Phenylphenol	Disinfectant, fungicide	Same as Phenol.
Phosphoric acid	Fertilizer, detergent, solvent, antioxidant	Mucous membrane and skin irritation.
Polyethylene glycol	Lubricant, emulsifying agent	None
Potassium hydroxide (See Sodium hydroxide)		
Propylene glycol	Preservative, emulsifier	None
PVP (polyvinyl pyrrolidone)	Dispersing and suspending agent, and as a lacquer in hair sprays.	Inhaled: enlarged lymph nodes, lung masses, and changes in blood cells; potential carcinogen.
Sodium benzoate	Food preservative	None
Sodium carboxymethyl-cellulose	Soil-suspending agent in detergents; stabilizing ingredient in foods; suspending agent and viscosity-increasing agent in drugs	None
Sodium cumenesulfonate	Disinfectant	None
Sodium hydrogen sulfate (sodium bisulfate)		See Sodium sulfate.
Sodium hydroxide (lye)	Drain cleaners, oven cleaners	Corrosive to all tissues.
Sodium hypochlorite	Bleaching agent	Inhaled: severe bronchial irritation, pulmonary edema; ingested: corrosion of mucous membranes, gastric perforation; skin irritation.

Substance	Use	Known Environmental/Health Effect
Sodium percarbonate	Bleaching agent	Mucous membrane and skin irritation.
Sodium perborate	Bleaching agent, antiseptic	Mucous membrane damage.
Sodium phosphate, dibasic	Emulsifier, control of acidity in foods and cosmetics	Mucous membrane and skin irritation; diarrhea; stimulates algae growth in waterways.
Sodium phosphate, monobasic	In baking powder, other foods	Stimulates algae growth in waterways.
Sodium phosphate, tribasic (trisodium phosphate)	Builder in detergents, water softener, clarifying sugar	Stimulates algae growth in waterways.
Sodium silicates	Preservative, fireproofing agent, adhesive, protective agent for washing machine parts	Mucous membrane and skin irritation; vomiting and diarrhea.
Sodium sulfate	Stabilizer in cleansers, detergents	Vomiting.
Surfactant	Generic term for detergents	Mucous membrane irritation.
Toluene	Solvent	Similar to benzene but less toxic.
1,1,1-Trichloroethane (methyl chloroform)	Solvent	Mucous membrane irritation; narcotic in high concentrations.
Trichloroethylene	Solvent, degreaser	Abnormal heart rhythms, symptoms like drunkenness, death.
Xylene	Solvent	Similar to benzene, but less toxic.
Xylenols	Disinfectant	None
Zinc chloride	Deodorant, disinfectant, wood preservative, antiseptic	Mucous membrane and skin irritant.

Mail-Order Catalog Listings

001 *The Allergy Store*, 7345 Healdsburg Ave. #511, Sebastopol, CA 95472, (800) 824-7163/(707) 823-6202

002 *Amberwood*, Rt. 1, Box 206, Milner, GA 30257, (404) 358-2991

003 *Aubrey Organics Catalog*, 4419 N. Manhattan Ave., Tampa, FL 33614, (813) 877-4186

004 *Carole's Cosmetics*, 3081 Klondike Ave., Costa Mesa, CA 92626, (714) 546-6706

005 *Come to Your Senses*, 321 Cedar Ave. S., Minneapolis, MN 55454, (612) 339-0050

006 *The Compassionate Consumer*, P.O. Box 27, Jericho, NY 11753, (718) 445-4134 ($1.00 catalog)

007 *Ecco Bella*, 6 Provost Sq., Ste. 602, Caldwell, NJ 07006, (800) 888-5320/(201) 226-5799

008 *The Ecology Box*, 425 E. Washington #202, Ann Arbor, MI 48104, (313) 662-9131

009 *Internatural*, P.O. Box 580, Shaker St., South Sutton, NH 03273, (603) 927-4776

010 *Janice Corporation*, 198 Rt.46, Budd Lake, NJ 07828, (800) 526-4237/(201) 691-2979

011 *Jason Natural Cosmetics*, 8468 Warner Dr., Culver City, CA 90232-2484, (800) 821-5791

012 *Jeanne Rose Herbal Body Works*, 219A Carl St., SanFrancisco, CA 94117, (415) 564-6785

013 *Kennedy's Natural Foods*, 1051 W. Broad Street, Falls Church, VA 22046, (703) 533-8484 ($2.00 catalog)

014 *Meadowbrook Herb Garden*, Route 138, Wyoming, RI 02898, (401) 539-7603

015 *Nature's Gate*, 9183-5 Kelvin Ave., Chatsworth, CA 91311, (800) 327-2012/(818) 882-2951

016 *Organic Farms/Smile Herb Shop*, P.O. Box 989, 4908 Berwyn Rd., College Park, MD 20740

017   *Sunrise Lane*, 780 Greenwich St., New York, NY 10014, (212) 242-7014

018   *Towards Life Catalog*, P.O. Box 2243, Yountville, CA 94599, (707) 944-0713

019   *Under the Apple Tree*, Butler Mt. Rd., Renick, WV 24966

020   *Weleda, Inc.*, 841 S. Main Street, Spring Valley, NY 10977, (914) 356-4134

021   *WSA Pharmacy*, 341 State St., Madison, WI 53703, (608) 251-3242

022   *Mountain Fresh Products*, P.O. Box 40516, Grand Junction, CO 81504.

023   *Nigra Enterprises*, 5699 Kanan Rd., Agoura Hills, CA 91301, (818) 889-6877

024   *Livos Plant Chemistry*, 614 Aqua Fria Street, Santa Fe, NM 87501, (505) 988-9111 for information; (800) 621-2591 for orders

025   *Auro Organic Paints*, Sinan Company, P.O. Box 181, Suisun City, CA 94585, (707) 427-2325

026   *AFM Enterprises*, 1140 Stacey Ct., Riverside, CA 92507, (714) 781-6860/6861

027   *Pace Chem Industries*, 779 La Grange Ave., Newbury Park, CA 91320, (805) 496-6224

028   *The Old Fashioned Milk Paint Co.*, Box 222, Groton, MA 01450, (617) 448-6336

029   *Murco Wall Products*, 300 NE 21st, Fort Worth, TX 76106, (817) 626-1987

030   *Negley Paint Co.*, P.O. Box 47848, San Antonio, TX 78265-8848, (512) 651-6996

031   *Allergy Relief Stop*, 2932 Middlebrook Pike, Knoxville, TN 37919, (615) 522-2795

032   *Baubiologie Hardware*, Box 51250, Ste. 125, Pacific Grove, CA 93950, (408) 372-8626

033   *Bloom's Ecological Consultants*, 25 Bonito Pl., Los Alamos, NM 87544, (505) 662-9007

034   *Flowright*, 1495 NW Gilman Blvd., Ste. 4, Issaquah, WA 98027, (206) 392-8357

035   *For Your Health Products*, 6623 Hillandale, Chevy Chase, MD 20815, (301) 654-1127

036   *The Home Zone*, 1038 Woodlawn, Grand Haven, MI 49417, (616) 847-0286

037   *Johnson Allergy Supply, Inc.*, 8101 Cedar Brook Dr., Louisville, KY 40219, (502) 966-0003

038   *The Living Source*, 3500 MacArthur Dr., Waco, TX 76708, (817) 756-6341

039 *Mountain Enterprises*, 3970 Pardes Way, Paradise, CA 95969, (916) 872-1994

040 *Natural Habitat*, 1626 Hansen St., Sarasota, FL 34231, (813) 924-6446

041 *N.E.E.D.S. (National Ecological & Environmental Delivery System)*, 120 Julian Place, Syracuse, NY 13210, (800) 634-1380/(315) 446-1122

042 *Nontoxic Alternatives*, 13 Ramona Dr., Orinda, CA 94563, (415) 376-6998

043 *Optimum Health*, 2449 E. 5th St., Long Beach, CA 90814, (213) 439-9819

044 *White Dolphin*, 218 F St., Eureka, CA 95501, (707) 445-2094

045 *Karen's Non Toxic Products*, P.O. Box 15, Malaga, NJ 08328, (800) 527-3674

046 *Young Oak Organic Landscape*, 632 Central Ave., Albany, NY 12206, (518) 458-2826

047 *The Body Shop*, 1341 7th St., Berkeley, CA 94710, (415) 524-0216

048 *Co-op America Catalog*, 2100 M St. NW, Ste. 310, Washington, DC 20063, (802) 658-5507

049 *Far Reaches—A Cottage Industry Catalog*, P.O. Box 151, Curlew, WA 99118

050 *Earthen Joys*, 1412 11th St., Astoria, OR 97103, (800) 451-4540

051 *In Harmony*, P.O. Box DDD, Albuquerque, NM 87196, (505) 345-5639

052 *Rosemary's Garden*, P.O. Box 1940, Redway, CA 95560, (800) 879-3337

053 *After the Stork*, 1501 12th St. NW, Albuquerque, NM 87104, (505) 243-9100

054 *Baby Bunz & Co.*, P.O. Box 1717, Sebastopol, CA 95473, (707) 829-5347

055 *Biobottoms*, P.O. Box 1060, 3820 Bodega Ave., Petaluma, CA 94953, (707) 778-7945

056 *Cuddlers Cloth Diapers*, 2500 24th St., Great Bend, KS 67530, (316) 792-6066

057 *Diap-Air*, 4003 Oglethorpe St., Hyattsville, MD 20782, (301) 277-5389

058 *Family Clubhouse*, 6 Chiles Ave., Asheville, NC 28803, (704) 254-9236

059 *Grandma's Best Diapers*, 218 State St., Carmi, IL 62821, (618) 684-2170

060 *Lovely Essentials*, St. Francis, KY 40062, (502) 865-5501

061 *Metrobaby*, P.O. Box 1572, New York, NY 10013-0869,

062 *The Motherwear Collection*, Box 114, Northampton, MA
     01061, (413) 586-3488

063 *The Natural Baby Company*, RD 1 Box 160S, Titusville, NJ
     08560, (609) 737-2895

064 *Richman Cotton Co.*, 529 Fifth St., Santa Rosa, CA 95401,
     (800) 992-8924; in Cal., (800) 851-2556/(707) 575-8924

065 *Soft As A Cloud*, 1355 Meadowbrook Ave., Los Angeles, CA
     90019, (213) 933-4417

066 *Traditions*, P.O. Box 409, Fairfield, IA 52556, (515) 472-6771

067 *The Vermont Country Store*, P.O. Box 3000, Manchester
     Center, VT 05255-3000, (802) 362-2400

068 *Portland Soakers*, P.O. Box 19827, Rochester, NY 14619

069 *WoolyBottoms*, 322 Wilson St., Albany, CA 94710, (415) 525-
     9355

070 *Naturpath Birthing Supply*, R.R. 1, Box 99C, Hawthorne, FL
     32640, (800) 542-4784/(904) 481-2821

071 *Rock-A-Bye Baby*, HCR 21 Box 50, Washington, VT 05675,
     (802) 883-5578

072 *Baby Biz*, P.O. Box 404, Eldorado Springs, CO 80025, (303)
     499-2469

073 *Classics for Kids*, P.O. Box 614, Silver Spring, MD 20901,
     (800) 882-KIDS

074 *Moonflower Birthing Supply*, P.O. Box 128, Louisville, CO
     80027, (303) 665-2120

075 *Autumn Harp*, 28 Rockydale Rd., Bristol, VT 05443, (802)
     453-4807

076 *Borlind's of Germany*, P.O. Box 1487, New London, NH
     03257, (603) 526-2076

077 *Granny's Old Fashioned Products*, P.O. Box 256, Arcadia, CA
     91006, (818) 577-1825

078 *Life Tree/Sierra Dawn*, P.O. Box 1203, Sebastopol, CA 95472,
     (707) 823-3920

079 *Allen's Naturally*, P.O. Box 339, Farmington, MI 48332-0339,
     (313) 453-5410

080 *Neway*, Little Harbor, Marblehead, MA 01945, (617) 631-9400

081 *Seventh Generation*, 10 Farrell St., So. Burlington, VT 05403,
     (800) 456-1177

082 *Home Service Products*, 230 Willow St., Bound Brook, NJ
     08805, (201) 356-8175

083 *Safer Products*, Oakmont Investment Co., 44 Oak St.,
     Newton Upper Falls, MA 02164, (617) 449-1580

084 *Ringer*, 9959 Valley View Road, Eden Prairie, MN 55344-
     3585, (800) 654-1047

085 *Necessary Trading Co.*, New Castle, VA 24127, (703) 864-5103

086 *Gardener's Supply*, 128 Intervale Rd., Burlington, VT 05401, (802) 863-1700

087 *Zook & Ranck*, RD1 Box 243, Gap, PA 17527, (717) 442-4171

088 *Gardens Alive*, Natural Gardening Research Center, Hwy 48, P.O. Box 149, Sunman, IN 47041, (812) 623-3800

089 *Bountiful Gardens*, Ecology Action, 5798 Ridgewood Rd., Willits, CA 95490

090 *Johnny's Selected Seeds*, Foss Hill Rd., Albion, ME 04910, (207) 437-9294

091 *Real Goods*, 3041 Guidiville Rd., Ukiah, CA 95482, (800) 762-7325

092 *New Alchemy Institute*, 237 Hatchville Rd., E. Falmouth, MA 02536, (508) 564-6301

093 *Natural Elements*, 145 Lee St., Santa Cruz, CA 95060, (408) 425-5448

094 *Bumkins Family Products, Inc.*, 7720 E. Redfield Rd., Scottsdale, AZ 85260, (800) 553-9302/(602) 483-7070

095 *Diaperaps*, P.O. Box 3050, Granada Hills, CA 91394 (800) 251-4321

096 *It's A Small World/Dappi Diaper Covers*, 417 San Antonio Ctr., Mt. View, CA 94040, (415) 949-4943

097 *The R. Duck Co.*, 650 Ward Dr., Suite H, Santa Barbara, CA 93111, 800-422-DUCK/(805) 964-4343

098 *Home Service Products*, 230 Willow St., Bound Brook, NJ 08805, (201) 356-8175

099 *Growing Naturally*, P.O. Box 54, 149 Pine Lane, Pineville, PA 18946, (215) 598-7025

100 *Dano Enterprises, Inc.*, 75 Commercial St., Plainview, NY 11803, (516) 349-7300

101 *Beauty Without Cruelty/Pamela Marsen, Inc.*, 451 Queen Anne Road, Teaneck, NJ 07666, (201) 836-7820

102 *Ida Grae Cosmetics/Nature's Colors, Ltd.*, 424 LaVerne Ave., Mill Valley, CA 94941, (415) 388-6101

103 *Warm Earth Cosmetics*, 334 W. 19 St., Chico, CA 95928

104 *Vegan Street*, P.O. Box 5525, Rockville, MD 20855, (800) 422-5525

105 *Nature Basics*, 61 Main St., Lancaster, NH 03584, (603) 788-4500

106 *Baudelaire*, Forest Rd., Marlow, NH 03456, (800) 327-2324

107 *All the Best*, 2713 E. Madison, Seattle, WA 98112, (800) 962-8266

108 *The Pet Connection*, P.O. Box 391806, Mountain View, CA 94039, (415) 949-1190

109 *Avena Botanicals*, P.O. Box 365, West Rockport, ME 04865, (207) 594-0694

110 *Sappo Hill Soapworks*, 654 Tolman Creek Rd., Ashland, OR 97520, (503) 482-4485

111 *Alexandra Avery*, 68183 Northrup Creek Rd., Birkenfeld, OR 97016, (503) 755-2446

112 *Alba Botanica Cosmetics*, P.O. Box 1858, Santa Monica, CA 90406, (213) 451-0936

113 *Simmons Handcrafts*, 42295 Hwy. 36, Bridgeville, CA 95526

114 *Heavenly Soap*, 5948 E. 30th St., Tucson, AZ 85711, (602) 790-9938

115 *The Real Aloe Co.*, P.O. Box 3428, Simi Valley, CA 93063, (800) 541-7809, (805) 522-5310

116 *Rainbow Research Corp.*, 170 Wilbur Place, Bohemia, NY 11716, (800) 722-9595, (516) 589-5563

117 *Kiss My Face Corp.*, P.O. Box 804, New Paltz, NY 12561, (914) 255-0884

118 *Walnut Acres*, Penns Creek, PA 17862, (800) 433-3998

119 *Sombra Cosmetics, Inc.*, 5600-G McLeod N.E. Albuquerque, NM 87109 (800) 225-3963, (505) 888-0288

120 *4-D Hobe, Inc.*, 201 S. McKemy St., Chandler, AZ 85226, (602) 257-1950

121 *The Right Start*, Right Start Plaza, 5334 Sterling Center Dr., Westlake Village, CA 91361, (800) 548-8531

122 *The Menstrual Health Foundation*, 2607 Marlow Rd., Santa Rosa, CA 95403, (707) 544-3876, (707) 792-2777

123 *Sisterly Works*, RR3 Box 107, Port Lavaca, TX 77979

124 *Lakon Herbals*, 4710 Templeton Rd., Montpelier, VT 05602, (802) 223-5563

125 *Jurlique-D'Namis Ltd.*, 16 Starlit Dr., Northport, NY 11768, (516) 754-3535

126 *Earth Science, Inc.*, P.O. Box 1925, Corona, CA 91718, (800) 222-6720, (714) 524-9277

127 *The Body Shop, Inc.*, 45 Horsehill Rd., Cedar Knolls, NJ 07927-2003, (800) 541-2535

128 *Auromere*, 1291 Weber St., Pomona, CA 91768, (714) 629-8255

129 *Carme, Inc.*, 84 Galli Dr., Novato, CA 94949, (415) 883-3367

130 *Aloegen Natural Products*, 9183-5 Kelvin Ave., Chatsworth, CA 91311, (800) 327-2012, (818) 882-2951

131 *Save-a-Tree*, P.O. Box 862, Berkeley, CA 94701, (415) 524-2253

132 *TreeSavers*, 249 S. Hwy. 101, Suite 518, Solana Beach, CA 92075, (619) 481-6403

133 *L.L.Bean*, Freeport, ME 04033, (800) 221-4221

About The Bennett Information Group

The Bennett Information Group is a consortium of experts in business and science. Executive director **Steven J. Bennett** has collaborated on more than 30 business management and computing books. He also has extensive experience as a science and medical writer. Mr. Bennett holds an M.A. from Harvard University in Regional Studies. For *The Green Pages*, Mr. Bennett was joined by the following experts:

Tom Maugh. Dr. Maugh researched and wrote the section introductions and the guide to environmental issues. He holds a Ph.D. in chemistry and is a science writer for the *Los Angeles Times* where he often writes about environmental issues.

Dorian Yates Kinder. Ms. Kinder served as the mail-order product consultant for *The Green Pages*. She owns and manages Pure Podunk, Inc., a manufacturer of non-toxic, chemical-free wool-filled bedding. She has worked for a number of environmental organizations as a researcher and writer.

June LaPointe. Ms. LaPointe conducted corporate and trade association research for the project. In addition to her professional research activities, she specializes in developing seminars on gathering competitor intelligence in the European Community.

Nancy Schmid. Ms. Schmid helped collect data from corporations and environmental organizations. She holds an MBA and serves as a free-lance researcher and analyst to small consulting groups.

You can write The Bennett Information Group at P.O. Box 1646, Cambridge, MA 02238.